THROUGH THE EYES OF A GEMINI

CRAIG V. TAYLOR JR.

Copyright © 2021 Craig V. Taylor, Jr.

All rights reserved. No part of this publication may be used or reproduced by any means, electronic, mechanical, graphic, including photocopying, recording, taping or by any information storage retrieval system or otherwise be copied for public or private use – other than "fair use" as brief quotations within articles and reviews – without prior written permission of the copyright owner.

ISBN: 978-1-954609-07-5

This book was printed in the United States of America

To order additional copies of this book contact:

LaBoo Publishing Enterprise, LLC
staff@laboopublishing.com
www.laboopublishing.com

ACKNOWLEDGEMENTS

I want to acknowledge my cousin, Kimmoly LaBoo, for helping me to bring my dream goal to life. Using LaBoo Publishing Enterprise allowed my dream to take flight. I also want to thank a friend and former co-worker, Martin Coleman, for drawing out my vision for this book cover. I remember multiple times asking for multiple changes because I was being a stickler for details. That'll be a laugh he and I will always share; but he's forever a good guy in my eyes.

For any feedback about the book:

Facebook: Cassiel Taylor
Instragram: 1King.2pawns

TABLE OF CONTENTS

Introduction 1
Hard to Read 5
Lost 6
Real Life 7
Free Write 8
Cold Fire 10
The Darkest Shadow 11
Lights Out 12
A Moment in Time 13
Unspeakable 14
And the Winner Is… 15
Out of Order 16
Beauty 17
Mechanical Heart 18
Love Council 19
Heart Racer 20
Friends with Benefits 21
Her Garden Guardian 22
Unconditional 23
Live for Today 24
Drama 25
Contagious 26
Cold 27
The Best Game Ever 28
I Miss You 30
Need and Wants 31
Seductive Eyes 33
Underrated MVP 34

Valentine All the Time	36
Body of Art	37
Through the Eyes of a Gemini	38
Love Knot	40
Father Times' Daughter	41
Christians in Disguise	43
Sex & Love Potions	45
Her Mind	47
Heart Eater	49
Wild Heart	51
Life's Bullets	54
L.A.S.T	55
Council Relapse	57
Metaphorically Speaking	60
Can't Stop	62
Hide and Seek	63
Presidential Collections	65
Verbally Unconscious	67
Shade	69
Shade 2	71
Brutality	74
Inside Man	76
Forward in Reverse	78
Incredible	80
Evolving	82
By My Side	84
Writer's Block	86
Primetime	88
Her Skin	90
Pages	92
Rekindle	94
Rich Minded	96

Ava's Eyes	98
M	101
A Fantasy Tease	103
Good Morning Moon	105
The Father in Me	107
Tot's Heart	109
Rebellious Rebel	111
H.O.E (Hell on Earth)	114
Jabs	117
These Eyes So Far	119
Reminiscing with Seduction	121
Fulsome Light	124
Her Rest	126
Normality	127
Senseless	129
Lifetime	132
Money Hereafter	134
Night Prowl	135
The Transparency	137
Everything Is Love	139
Love for Generations	141
The Motions	142
Edible Foreplay	144
Years Ahead	146
Blind Eye Murder	148
Talk 'n Text	150
Family Come Up	152
Special Delivery	154
Day in a Life: Zelda	157
Food Porn	159
Psychological Test	161
No Days Off	164

The Temple	166
Safekeeping	168
The Franchise	170
Daddy's Girl	172
Joker	174
Rumors	176
Pencil Thin	178
Love at War	180
Pay the Teller	182
Then & Now	183
Taylor Son	187
Entertainment	190
Writer's Block 2: Low Ink	192
Humble Karma	194
Home Free	196
More Life	198
Why Lie?	200
Small Circle, Low Blows	202
Cold Turkey	204
Purify	206
Dear Mae	209
Entitlement	211
Remember Me	213
Free Game	215
Zombie Shift	217
Yeezy Taught Me	219
Take Flight	223
Peace for Ransom	224
Motivated to Help	227
Depression	229
This Is It	231
Well Done	232

INTRODUCTION

One of my many goals in life was to publish, and now I can proudly say that I was able to accomplish that. I can only thank God for positioning me to be able to publish my creativity. This has been a long time coming, dating back to when I was still in high school. A decade's worth of writing all in one book. Before I go any further into about what this book is about, I must mention what caused me to start this poetic writing journey that you'll soon be reading.

Growing up as an only child, I had to learn quickly how to entertain myself. Of course, while I was home, I had toys, video games, and television; but while attending school, I had to use other methods whenever my work was completed. In no time, I began writing my own page-long stories using my favorite cartoons to unfold my imagination. I also began drawing my own personal comics and making up my own superhero characters. My close friends and family that I attended school with enjoyed them and made sure they gave me all different kinds of feedback. Even though my drawings were only stick figures at the time, it was the storyline that kept them asking for more comic drawing material.

As I began my middle school years, my mindset began to shift back to writing, only this time I wanted to write a full novel. I challenged myself to do one, and as I started, I knew I had what it took to finish it. But once I able to finish the climax portion of the novel, I was unable to get myself to finish out the rest of it. Because of that, I somewhat lost my confidence to keep writing, as I decided to go back to drawings and comics. I knew I wanted to do better than stick figures, so when I had art class, I started looking into drawing anime characters out of this Manga book I used to read. It properly taught me how to draw and exploring more details within the drawings. When I entered my last year in middle school, music began to be a big motivator for me. I would listen to all kinds of music, just so I could feel the vibes of whatever the artist intended for the listener to hear, but most of the time I would be listening to hip hop. I listened to it so much, I even started writing my own raps and songs, even though I knew they were funny and corny. It just helped me to expand my mind in writing since I wasn't doing much after the unfinished novel I attempted to do.

As high school unfolded, I really didn't have much of a motive to do anything writing or drawing related my first-year in. I can only assume that I was too busy trying to adapt and adjust to new schooling and trying to make new friends. I began writing again during my sophomore year. It was an emotional day I was having. I didn't want to talk to anyone about it, but I was tired of thinking and feeling the way that I was; so, I wrote it out. At this time, I didn't know very much about poetry, but once I read it, it seemed somewhat poetic. Writing out how I felt was both therapeutic and artistic in my eyes, so I began looking more into poetry and attempted to make this consistent for me. When my junior year came along, I took a poetry class and journalism class. The poetry class helped me to understand different poetry styles and flow. The journalism class was also a part of the school's newspaper, so if I ever had an opportunity to show the school my material, then this would be the class and opportunity I would need to do so. While attending journalism class, I attempted to learn all I could learn about publishing news articles with the school's newspaper, along with keeping up with school's sports section, the after-school programs, and whatever important bulletins and school plays that were soon to start. Even though I kept up with all that, I still found time to do my own writing because I wanted to have my work in the school newspaper.

My opportunity to post my material in the school's newspaper didn't come until the very end of my senior year. It was post-graduation and most of the seniors, like myself, were gone and really didn't have to attend school. The school paper didn't have much left to report since the school year was pretty much over, so I approached my journalism teacher and suggested my poetry and she approved it. After the paper was out for some time, I started to get approached by different students, and teachers that were reading the paper and wanted to give me positive feedback on the poems in the paper. Even our principal, at that time, came to me and gave me praise and feedback. She told me that she wished she had the opportunity to teach me in her English Honors class. During this time in school, my principal was also an English teacher. English Honors is basically a class for students that excel highly in this course and were ready for college material. After hearing her tell me this, I only wished I had the opportunity to attend her class, to challenge myself with my writing limitations, but it was way too late. Despite being late, this shifted my mind to publish on a more global scale. To share my work with others and see what other potential possibilities could be out there for me. If I can say one thing to anyone that's chasing a dream, I'd say to continue to press forward no matter what stands in your way. You never know who's out there waiting for you to maximize those dreams into reality as you stretch beyond all limitations to impact the lives of others.

Within these pages are a series of transitions as boy becomes man, husband, and a father. At the end of the day, I am human. I've lived and learned through many flaws, mistakes, and problems. I have witnessed a lot of good and blessings in my 27 years of living thus far. At times, I treated my poetry like a diary or journal, and other times it's been used simply for the art of storytelling; but it's real, it's raw, it's entertaining. Enjoy.

HARD TO READ

Life can sometimes be like a piece of paper

You may be balled up

Kicked around

Or even ripped up

But if no one can read how you really feel, then you might as well stay blank

(2013)

LOST

Searching, for something that can't be found

Looking, for something that can't be seen

Trapped, in a secret that I couldn't keep away

Misunderstood, by the people that already know me

(2011)

REAL LIFE

This will be my last time here

I'm going to cut the umbilical cord right here

And walk into this world as a free man

Setting the bar high, with a good plan

Adulthood is about to slap me in the face

Reality is setting in, but I'm ready for a good race

Once the gun fires, I'm setting the pace

Because there isn't a second chance to get it right

No more being bossed, it's time to boss up

The world is a big business, I'm just trying to entrepreneur it

Real life is starting to settle in

But it's up to me whether I make it seem easy or hard

(2011)

FREE WRITE

I write to correct the wrong

To speak the truth, but not to form a song

I write to light up the dark

To give you truth and courage, to inject in your heart

I write to express love and free mind

I write about how good life can be

To dream and set your goals

To face the world for what it is and be bold

I write to help heal the world, and enrich the poor

To bring race together and restore

To help anyone who needs a hand

To bring order so everyone can understand

I write to wipe the tears away

To help people in the hospital fight another day

I write to unlock the cages and erase the pain

Because everything I have lost in life, will help me to gain

I write to strengthen my mind with knowledge

To make sure this blessing does not go to waste

I write to be known

That I am a nobody, trying to be somebody in this world

I write to create my own history

So that each day I live, I make it my best

I write what I want

These words are the key to unlocking a whole new state of mind

So, I free write to keep my mind free

(2010)

COLD FIRE

Hot as the sun

Cold as the night

I can describe myself as both

I can love someone with a passion

But can't feel a true vibe between them and I

I don't know which side suits me most

I love to hate

And hate to love

I'm as dark as a secret

And as bright as gold

I display cold fire

(2010)

THE DARKEST SHADOW

You were always with me, but not beside me

You only move when I move, but do not make a sound

When I cry, you do not make a sound

In the light, you move just like me

In the dark, I am alone

You can see me, but I can't see you

With no choice of words, you stare at me in the night

You're not good, but you're not bad either

You're just there

Watching and moving as I do

As much as I ignore you, you're always watching me in silence

(2010)

LIGHTS OUT

What will you do when the darkness begins to sin?

When death bleeds chaos which seems to never end

As love and peace slowly begins to lose the battle with war

And Mother Nature kills us all slowly from the Earth's core

Death comes quietly and offers no cure

Keeping its promise to never be pure

And love always seems to be lost in sin and desire

But hope seems to be our last resort

The weapon that reaches no limit

As we fall to our knees on this cold and heartless ground

Clamp our hands as our state of mind creates no sound

And make peace with ourselves through prayer

Closing our eyes

Cutting our sight of pain into our darkness of faith

(2011)

A MOMENT IN TIME

It seemed like what we had could've lasted forever

But forever turned into years

Years then turned into months

Months turned into days

Days soon turned into hours

And hours made their way down to minutes

And within no time, minutes became a matter of seconds

So where are we now?

What is there left to tell?

(2011)

UNSPEAKABLE

I'm up late because you're running through my mind

Wishing I could take you back, but I've already been left behind

Remembering what we once was

But now I have no control anymore

I can't sleep without you being in my dreams

I can't speak without mentioning the way you used to look at me

I'm speaking the unspeakable because you don't care anymore

While you're running away from our love

I'm running for you, trying to save us before its unfixable

Don't you see I'm shedding these tears for you?

Don't you even see me like you used to see me?

Fate is pulling me back to you, but you do not seem to see

I have given you all the signs

Now I am waiting to see if you can read them

What was lost can be restored

All that I offer is waiting on you

(2010)

AND THE WINNER IS...

Our love would have been out of this world

Too bad you never even gave me a chance

You left me before I could even get to know you

You back-stabbed me before I could even feel the pain

Numbing my own pain to better understand yours, now I'm rewarded with twice the pain

You ran away, with no goodbyes, and didn't even care

But don't worry I've closed the door on you

And chained it shut

There is no need for me to explode in rage

I'm just going to applaud at your ignorance

You and I could have been all we wanted

But you've made your decision

And it's permanent like a tombstone

And when it's all said and done

The Jerk of The Year Award goes to you

You are the winner

But there isn't a standing ovation

(2011)

OUT OF ORDER

Everything is gone

I'm all dried up

I'm all out of smiles

And my love has vanished

I can't explain what is wrong with me

I feel like a machine

Just use me until nothing is left

Cold and heartless, I'm easy to use

I don't know how to explain it

I know something is wrong

Maybe I'm just out of order

(2010)

BEAUTY

We've played a long game of hide and seek

But in the end, we always find each other

It took me a long time to figure you out

But I took the time to do so

Your name is hard to describe because it is more than what it is

It's further than love and stronger than strength

We always stood beside each other, but it always seemed as if I was the opposite of you

But you had guided me to a path where my eyes couldn't

And shared with me your side

No longer do I have to hide from you

We can share the same life

As we walk together, until our feet bleed

Painting a perfect picture of you and I

Like I said, your name is far more than what it stands for

But for now, it's beauty

(2010)

MECHANICAL HEART

Excuse me for being a gentleman

But I can't help this feeling that you've always been a part of me

Your face and outgoing beauty, keeps my heart at ease

Your texture and grace of style blow me away

My heart races out of control when you're near

As if our hearts are somewhat connected

And every time my heart seems out of whack, it seems you're always nearby to ease it

No other person can read my expressions and my heart like you can

I just want to be with you, so just take my hand

Come share with me a long dance

Until our hearts are one

And as I look into your eyes, I know we will always escape the pain from our past

And toss it aside like broken glass

You're the one that completes me

You're the thing that keeps my heart alive

Because it only beats for you

(2011)

LOVE COUNCIL

When we came to be, I thought we would just be friends

But as we began to talk and laugh, this became a real case

Friendship was in the courtroom, and love was the judge

We endured the trail and handled the trials

Our friendship became a relationship as the gavel banged

And now I can't stop staring at this beauty I've claimed

As I promise to never let you go

People may say that she's not perfect, but she's perfect for me and that's what mattered

From this day forward, I'll always remember the girl named Council

That always keeps my heart pure

No matter what condition it may be in

My heart is hers to keep

(2011)

HEART RACER

Candle lit room, she looks at me

I hold her tight as we lay in bed

We hold, we kiss

She touches me, I tighten my grip

She scratches, I kiss

She moans, I sweat

I look in her eyes, she bites her lip

Enjoying the feeling as love is being made

Bed rocking, tears dropping

Breathing hard, my chest is knocking

As if my heart is ready to burst out of my chest

It finally comes to an end. I go back to looking into her eyes

I'm out of breath as she catches her breath

Laying together, we're looking deeply into each other's eyes until the candles no longer gave light

(2011)

FRIENDS WITH BENEFITS

It started as just a small and unnoticed friendship

But months and days went by, it began to grow into something more

In my eyes, I see more

As I approach you now, I'm calmer and humbler around you

With a smile that brightens any day, and the looks to blow the sun out

When I see that you are in pain, or stressed, I'm willing to put my life on the line to just make sure you stay happy

Because every time you're in need of help

A laugh, support

A person to listen and understand you

Someone to ease your pain

A person that brightens your day

Or even a simple hug

I want to be the one you would want to turn and rely on

With both sleeves full of emotions, I am willing to cater to your every need

(2012)

HER GARDEN GUARDIAN

Roses are red, so is her dress

As cute as she can be, she is truly blessed

But dare not touch, beware of her thorns

Having to choose my words carefully, I don't have her thorns to prick me

Very little height, but always bright

Her smile blinds me every time she's in my sight

My hope for her is to remain red, and never to be black

I don't want this to be a temporary forever

If she wanted a bed to grow and help her spread out, then she's in mine

If I must be her vase of water, then I'll keep her wet

If she needs warmth, then I'll be her sun

Anything I can do to keep her right, then I'm willing to be her gardener

(2013)

UNCONDITIONAL

Today I shall create an oath with you

The day I came to you

And confess my emotions and problems and expose my wounds

Knowing that I'm not alone, you are here to assist me as I manage to help you

With a friendship being stitched together, our feelings are shown

And in the end, love leaves a permanent mark

The path we chose wasn't what we wanted, but it ended with us being together

What lies ahead may not be easy, but as long as we are stitched together, then nothing can tear us apart

What people say can't hurt us

What people do won't stop us

They can try but it won't lead to success

They want what we have

But they simply cannot

Because what we have is unconditional

(2013)

LIVE FOR TODAY

Life

It has its ups and downs

Bills, taxes, and unresolved problems

I sit back and look back at the world and ask myself

Where did it all go?

Fun, laughter, and adventure

Is it simply because I grew up?

Or maybe because life became more serious

I don't know where it might have gone, but I want it back

I want every day to be the best day ever

Laugh, party, take a trip around the world maybe, and enjoy the sun's rays

Enjoy the love of friends and family as stress becomes a distraction

Some people prefer to go through the hardship and pain to get to where I'm saying

But I'd rather live for today because tomorrow isn't promised to no one

I'd rather live it up now

But not just for now

But forever

(2014)

DRAMA

I never knew how it started or how it began

But I know you keep finding a way back every time I find a way out

You're like the air I breathe and the water I drink

You're like a spider web and I'm the fly trapped in it

I can't escape

You have gripped and clinched yourself to my life

As frustration and stress increases, my mind gives me unneeded and unwanted memories that I thought were gone

And in return, I hurt the wrong people as I begin to lose a piece of myself

As if my puzzle is slowly taking itself apart

If I could go back in time and find the source of you, I would end it all

But now, I can only manage as I figure a way to escape or finish this mess, I've put myself in

But I would hope you wouldn't drag me back once I find a way out

I don't need you holding me back anymore

Free bird life, I'm not used to cages

(2014)

CONTAGIOUS

I don't know what you did to me, but you left me wanting more

You have my full attention and now I can't keep away from you

I try to move on and get away, but you have me hypnotized

I simply can't get away

You continue to exercise my brain

And I simply can't get you out my damn mind

It drives me crazy how you have me trapped and only wanting more of you

Always by my side and never leaving me alone

Running away isn't an option

And staying with you is only bittersweet

You're worse than breaking a habit and you kill me more than drugs

Stuck with many unanswered questions, you leave me with no cure

(2014)

COLD

I am cold

I am cold hearted

I do not warm for no one

So, let me allow myself to be frozen

At one point I used to be warm

My feelings were too

But they were burned by the summer's heat

And soon fell apart during the fall

Leaving them to freeze in the winter

The more I think about you, the more my fingers go numb and turn blue

As my brain freezes and my body shakes for warmth

Deep within my soul is a small flame on its dying breath as hard snow and ice surrounds it

I guess this qualifies me as a man of ice

Or a cold soul in a dead body

I am cold

I hope I don't give you chills

(2014)

THE BEST GAME EVER

I didn't make this game, I was only born and raised to play it

I didn't know how to play at first

People around me knew what they were doing, while others didn't

I watched and learned over and over how to play but it was only practice and learning from the pros

After a certain age, I began to figure it out

It took some years, but I became a pro amongst the masters

I thought I was good enough to beat the system

The power I thought I had to win it all slipped through my hands

I got caught cheating

I thought I had everything planned out

That I cracked the code to this game as a pro instead of patiently waiting to be a master

I got caught; busted

I lost and the restart button was broke

I was a pro and now I'm back at learning the game

I became the rest that didn't succeed

The game has control of me now

Telling me to keep playing despite me cheating

Whether I ignore the game or not, people around will be a constant reminder

This game is a devil's trap

And I was introduced to it without a choice

But the only way to beat the system is to keep playing

Because players never stop playing

(2014)

I Miss You

One sentence, three words, eight letters

I miss you

I don't know what it is you do to me to make me miss you

It could be that smile that helps me have a brighter day

Or it just might be the love you offer me

You are a friend and a best friend, and I miss you when we are not near

You are the yin to my yang

Did you get my "I miss you" text? Did it come through?

I know it wouldn't be a group message because it was only for me and you

About how I truly care and miss you

My buddy, my best friend, my lover, my comfort zone

When you are near, I am bliss

When you're gone, it's far too long

I miss you; I miss you

And I love you when I'm not missing you

(2014)

NEED AND WANTS

I need you

I lust and desire you

You satisfy things I never craved before

And leave me only wanting more

I need for us to be together forever

If forever seems fair

I want us

I want your time, love, and patience

I want sex

The general and the rough

The holding, the moaning, and the crying

I need the support

And I want the arguments

Only to make up and make love in the end

I want to be your backbone and the support you first saw in me

And for it to never change us

If I change and do not realize it, then help me

Fighting with and for me

I don't want to lose us

We are all we have in one another

I love you

I want us to be forever like time

(2014)

SEDUCTIVE EYES

My body is tangled in a chain of thought

And my mind has detached itself from me on to you

The proper path I was on changed route when I saw you

Those eyes

Seductive, are they not?

The look you gave me makes my spine curl

My mind is losing this battle as my body wants to challenge how dangerous you can be

Use me

Defile my body

Take every dose of me until we are both desire

Finish me up

Those eyes ignited something within me that wasn't supposed to happen

But the danger in me is now fearless

Those eyes are weapons of mass seductions

(2014)

UNDERRATED MVP

For years I've been a part of a team

Giving my all to a supporting cast that lacks teamwork

Putting in time and sacrificing my mind and body

Not for me, but for us

Season after season players came and went

I've taught, I've guided, I stayed consistent

I've played different roles and positions, and challenged myself for positions I knew I would excel at

But what makes me underrated is because I was never given those big chances

For a long time, I was thinking about us when everybody else was thinking about themselves

Teamwork is dead

This team is and always has been broken

Not one time did I feel like a simple thank you ever impacted me in a happy manner

This whole time I was a one-man army; as my body of work has been swept under the carpet

But no more

I will not be taken for a fool no more

Not only am I putting my foot down, I'm slamming it onto the floor

People telling me I shouldn't change to make myself a better player

That I'm better off being regular like everybody else

That was a cheap shot at my bosses, managers and agents; we aren't on good terms anymore

I want to be on a team that wants to be a team, and this isn't it

So, I'm cutting my contract short; this is my final year

Hopefully when I'm gone, you'll all see how big an impact player I really was

That I was always deserving of the MVP award

But business is business and maybe I'll always go unnoticed until I leave for something better

But when I'm gone, I'm gone

Always keep me in your memories

Because the best is hard to replace

(2014)

VALENTINE ALL THE TIME

Why celebrate my love for you on one day?

I love you every day

So why not be my valentine every day

We play together, we laugh together

We even sleep and wake up together

So why can't you be my cute cupid every day?

I love you every second my heart beats

Our love is sealed tighter than envelopes, closer than tar on the road, and hotter than the earth's core

You rock my world and generate earthquakes with your profound beauty

I don't have a valentine for one day

I have you for life

And I have the chance to celebrate that every day

Valentine's day is great

But you are a day within itself

Shining bright as the sun and glowing as big as the moon

You give me life

And I will never stop loving you for that

Because I love you

(2014)

BODY OF ART

This is my body

This is my temple

What I choose to do with it is for me to judge and no one else

This body alone has been through bumps and bruises

Has bled and cried

But this body is art

This body is strong

This is my sword and shield

The beauty of pain I present to it is art I use to push my body to it limits

Every day I live and breathe is a new day

To present the art of my body to a world that is a blank piece of paper

(2014)

THROUGH THE EYES OF A GEMINI

Through the eyes of a Gemini

You shall see bittersweet

Entertainment and boredom

Love and hate

There is no equal balance when it comes to us

Either accept our strangeness or move on

We don't live for perfection

We'd gamble life if we had the chance

Gone like the wind, there is no slowing us down

Only catching up or staying behind

Being mean isn't in my nature, I thrive on levels of humanism

Don't push beyond our boundaries

Don't try to deprive me of me

Don't try to change one that's consistently changing themselves

I am my own novel

But don't try to read me because not everything about me makes sense

And I don't stick to the script

Most of my work can be subliminal because not everything is worthy of being obvious due to personal feelings

Like a stick-shift, the speed is in our control

Just give us a clear lane, please

At the end of the day, as unbalanced as I am

As crazy and unequal as I can be

My heart is big and open

And like a fairy tale, I'm waiting for the right one to unlock the cage and set my heart free

A lot of people from the past thought they had the key, but the door still seems closed

Having me is like having a test

You can't pass or fail until I approve it

No matter what face you get out of me, it will be 100%

But the impact you have on my heart will determine what type of path you and I will have

So which path is destined for you?

(2014)

LOVE KNOT

This is my vow to you

As we tie and intertwine with one another

Tying together dreams, happiness, hopes, and unconditional love

May this knot never find a way to be untied

That no one interferes with what we made

We've worked hard to get to where we are today

And on this day, I will say "I love you"

That you are mine

Now and forever

We are a knot of love

No matter what happens, this knot is forever

I know our path isn't clear, and there will always be roadblocks

But whatever we run into, we'll handle it together

I just want us to stay in love, be tough, and strong for one another for many days to come, like a knot

(2015)

FATHER TIMES' DAUGHTER

She was born from a mixture of time and nature

Her purpose was never to honor Mother and Father's wishes

But to disobey

Some may say she is a blessing and a curse

Some may say her existence is a cold one

And others would rather stay away from her altogether

Her abilities are both godly and devilish, depending on what your views are of her

She likes to punish the people of earth

Some people live for all the wrong reasons

And some are just living, but not living right

But she catches their lies and exposes people with no warning

Through lies, cameras, social media, technology, or other people

She treats all our lies and disapproving actions as cases, like a detective

And in the end, she always wins

She knows all the clues and who to look for

There's no running away, everything she does takes time

Some of the cases she takes on might be done sooner rather than later

And other times, she just might have to wait it out

But all of them will be finished

She is the one that caused fate to exist

And fate is something you can never run from

So, live a clean slate

Or face the wrath of Karma

(2015)

CHRISTIANS IN DISGUISE

Some people like to play Christian

Some people like to act holy

God sees and hears all

And it isn't a pleasant sight to see

It's funny how some people like to reinforce their ways of belief on people

Or how people say "our way of living" is frowned upon by God

Then turn around and act the opposite of what they said, and act up behind closed doors and away from church

The same people that put on a show for Sunday

That their week's worth of sin can be corrected on a Sunday, and apologize, but not faithfully, and think it's all okay

You can't choose to turn your beliefs on and off like a switch

Either you are fully committed or not

I know what I am

I am a sinner

It's something I'm not fully proud of

But I am

But I'd rather be a sinner before I act or play around with the ways of the bible and Christianity

In due time, I will make the proper change

To live the correct life consistently

But right now, my life is a grind

And whatever opportunity comes my way for success, I'm willing to give it my all

To do what I can so I can live

But my time of change is coming soon

(2015)

SEX & LOVE POTIONS

You appeared in my life without any warning or hesitation

And gave me some love potion for my aching heart

I liked you in return, but you wanted love from me

So, you cast a spell on me

I already liked you

But that all evolved into more

My love used to be clouded and closed from the world

Now it's bright and open

And like a wide receiver, you gave me a pass and I was ready to score

So, when the night is dull and the moon is bright

And you're home alone calling me and saying where I can be tonight

That's when I'll capitalize on what your spell has done to me

Coming over, no words are exchanged

Just biting and kissing, as clothes come off

Laying you across the bed while your favorite love song

is stuck on repeat

For the lust that's filling up the room was never meant to be discreet

Laying in the bed, skin exposed

I'm grabbing, rubbing, and touching all the right areas

And kissing, licking, and sucking all the right spots

You're serving me my favorite dish, now watch me as I eat it up

Climax is the mountain and we are racing to the top

The moans flow stroke for stroke

And the way you say my name sounds as if you're exhausted from satisfaction

As the night turns into morning

I'm waking up to you cuddled under me

Missing the desire of your eyes, I stroke and play in your hair as you slowly wake up to reveal those lustful eyes

I'm not sure what this day will present, but bewitched or not, I'm glad to be with you

Hopefully this can be for a lifetime, if that's enough time for you

(2015)

HER MIND

Her mind started off as a maze

And I was just a memory in my own personal corner

But I decided to expand and explore

I tapped into her life

Her hobbies, her flaws

Her pain, her emotions

Soon her mind was focused around me

Throughout her workday, while she's with her friends, when we're not near each other, on her way to bed, and when she's first waking up

Staying in contact, seeing me, hearing my voice, all brings her closer to peace

Her mind started off as a maze I was confined in

But I made it into a candle

My existence in her life sparked the flame

I soon became the top thing on her mind, as I watched her mind melt away

I played all her mind games, but it was all structured by my rules

Now I have her mind for 24 hours

I've become the tattoo branded on her brain

I am here to stay

I thought you knew

(2015)

HEART EATER

I like to think I have superpowers

But I'm no superhero; just normal human qualities

I just use them to the best of advantage

Lust, temptation, desire, attention, and consistency are my gifts

Just looking for the right one to use it on

Some people like to put up a fight and think with their head

I avoid the brain and knock at the door of the heart

The brain likes to play checkers to rule me out the game

But chest is my perfection and I've always declared myself the winner

I treat the heart like a recipe

Sprinkle a little lust

Add extra time, attention, and desire

Mix it with a lot of temptation and consistency for extra flavor

Then let it bake in the oven they think it's love

Allowing the heart to warm up to it where I want it to be

When the time is right, and the heart is where I want it to

be, I'll separate our bond with a silver platter and serve your heart to myself

I'll use your bones as my fork and knife

Have her thinking to herself

"How could I be so foolish? How could I be so blindsided?"

The answer is simple: I allowed your heart to do the unthinkable, which was to think

Not only are you heartbroken, but now you're heartless

Leaving your brain to think you were in love

Thinking you were the one, you were just another one

I ate your heart right out of your chest for my own personal pleasures

Good luck finding a new one

(2015)

WILD HEART

I'm not here to butter you up

I'm not here out of patience

I want you and you want me

So, let's do this

I want you to use and abuse me like drugs

I'm here to give you a good fix

I want you closer than lotion being absorbed into my skin

Toss me on the bed, give me a show

Show me your favorite dance as clothes drop onto the floor

Crawling onto the bed

Aiming closer to me, I see the desire in your eyes

Skin touching, body temperature rising

Might want to check my temperature, I wouldn't want to get sick on you

For tonight we'll get wild like a rodeo show

Grab your strongest saddle and reverse cowgirl this bull

Hum your favorite tune, moan to the strokes and motions

Scream my name as if it's all my fault

Yell like you're in pain, but you know it feels good

Let your heart race and run wild like a heart attack that's reached untamed pleasures

Work up a sweat like you're running a marathon

And just before you tire out, I'll help you finish your race

Thrusting and rocking you

Like you're climbing to the peak of a rollercoaster before it drops

Don't close your eyes, let the lustful adrenaline in the air keep you up right a little longer before it blows you over

Falling over

Palm, grip, and grabbing the sheets for the show isn't over

Your legs may be out of commission but my leg is still going strong

It's the 12th round, the last lap, the final countdown

As the sun begins to rise, everything is in overdrive as our hearts are beating out of our chest for freedom

Everything speeding up but the atmosphere is in slow motion

Until everything releases and resets back to its normal sense

Sleeping the day away, waiting for the normal heart rate to return

I am nonexistent to the world

But when the night presents itself again

I will return and this time I'll let you be the captain

Riding the waves of you until you waterfall

Now that's wild

(2016)

LIFE'S BULLETS

Life

It's a never-ending gun show

Every now and then you can dodge some bullets

And other times you just must bite them

But the blood and pain you receive, you take it as a learning lesson

Let it be a weakness you turn into strength

So, when life throws you another curve

You can listen to the bullets whistle by as you dodge them every time

(2016)

L.A.S.T

Life as a sinner trending

Spreading like fire; born out of fresh air

Blessed by natural beauty, but praising the wrong idols

Worshiping man-made things

Survival is a thing of the past, because tomorrow is the new now

Savages and demons rule and possess us without our knowledge

We invite them without them asking

And in return, they give us greed, improper love, temporary sensations and life-ending power

Money becomes the new bible because it reads "In God We Trust"

We fight, sacrifice, and fiend for this green every day to live every day, just to repeat the process the next day

We abuse sex like drugs and kill new life like Earth's global warming

Hell on earth isn't just a saying, it's a true statement

We practice fighting religiously and pray less often

Assuming a blessing will rain down when troubles have reached a critical point

Only to come up empty on faith like a dry hydrant; just to slip back to a desert trail of sin as your soul dries up and dies from the overbearing sun

We fight, bleed, and try to survive like wolves

But the pack stays small because trust's leash can't seem to make it past two inches

Family and friends are divided and often die as emotions remain at a bone chilling cold

Sinners are trending like the world wide web

One click can leave you faithless as we follow each other like Twitter

The Basic Instructions Before Leaving Earth has changed to: Sinners Are Victimizing Each-other Daily

So basically, we've been S.A.V.E.D

Only in search of higher power

Our death has no heaven

Because our love and faith aren't where they belong

Heaven is supposed to be the finish line to our marathon

But the way things are now, we don't even deserve last place

(2016)

COUNCIL RELAPSE

Time went by

Years went by

And now I'm in a new era in my life

The love council we once were, is a long-distance memory now

The fumes and texture were worth it at the time, but we're in a different time zone now

In two different states, with two different people

The memories were deep and the love was genuine

Young at the time, fun and adventure was the objective

Sex was the top that opened the jar of emotions

As we all assumed this was real

The dances, the kisses, the outings and work—school combination were so worth it

The drives, the late-night rides and talks

How things could be for us in the future

Damn, time has changed

We appeared back in court; to the love judge

The gavel was slammed

And at an instant, everything that was united, split apart

Now all the bridges have burned

The old has rotted away and out came a new us, but the path is divided

Things just didn't seem right anymore as maturity began to set in

And we were no more

Every now and then I see a small glimpse of what we used to be

I guess you can say you was the best of all time at the time though

You gave me the best years of my life right before I branched out

In the end, pain was never supposed to come to you

The ending ended wrong

I guess I didn't practice my role enough to get it right in real time

Time gave us some distance

But as bad as my eyes are, I still see you on the horizon

I can't say I want the love back, because that would be a mistake

I only want to resolve the time we allow to pass without correcting what went wrong

But we are too far off to try to come back now

All I can do is think about it and write away

No pain, no guilt

Only a person that reminisces of what could have been a better outcome

It would have been better

Much, much better

(2016)

Metaphorically Speaking

There's a price we all must pay

Hell is on earth

But also, within the minds of ourselves

I'm just one of many that has the ability to present my devils

Dancing and playing in the dark, because the light burns my skin

A heart heartless, but only beats for sensational desires

Cold personality but the words I speak bring warmth to others

Consistently wearing shades because the hate constantly blinds and burns my eyes

My work is never clean because my hands stay dirty

I'm heaven sent but my facts are devilish

Life is a deck of cards, but I'm the joker no one wants to play

Stay swerving in my dream car because my reality is brakeless

I want people to inhale me like weed smoke and let the fumes be my soul that leaves you breathless

Let my business be finger scan safe so everybody knows not to touch what can't be keyed

Staying awake 24/7 because dreams can't be reached if you're dreaming your dreams

The stench of success comes naturally if you work hard enough to consistently achieve it

But my success smells like roses burning in a flower patch

Acting like love is all real, but once upon a time we all pretended

Treating girls like games until players are caught cheating

Old tricks get caught, but act like its brand new

Drugging her with lies, as they stack nosebleed high

But soon baby drama brings new life, so he can't seem to end his own

A demon raising an angel is the new milestone

Hell on earth is what she'll endure

As her path journeys into a series of yin yang metaphors

(2016)

CAN'T STOP

It began as a hurricane on judgement day

But then you came and struck me with your love

And had me trapped like lightning in a bottle

We started off as cuddle puddle love

But eventually we flash-flooded over and drowned in unconditional

Others tried to weather my storm, but they came and went quicker than a summer breeze on a dry day

They never saw the pain and hate I had while covering my tears in the rain

But your approach was as bright as a sunny day with a rainbow cape

Saving me with sun rays, so I can have a brighter day

Keeping my mind clear and away from clouded thoughts

And now, I'm happy like a bumble bee with just a minor sting

And my love is permanent like the four seasons

And like the weather, it can't be stopped

(2016)

HIDE AND SEEK

The truth isn't hiding, it's in plain sight

The things kept discreet during the day became confessions in the night

Burying all your lies, I soon dug up the truth

Backstabbing me with tacks, instead of knives, you're robbing me of all my youth

Dirty fingers grabbing jewels and up in your pride

Fulfilling your needs and pleasuring the deep loneliness inside

A queen waits for her king in the castle alone

Only to reveal herself like a dog to the knight so he can throw you a bone

As a pirate, this is supposed to be my treasure

But you're showing off your gold to miners as if you're a gold mine

The love is there, but respect must be in space

I'm writing us in forever's, but the thesis keeps getting deleted

Wanting fairy tales and happily ever after's

But reading in between you, I only see chapters of mystery

Trying to be a guard dog, but what use am I if my fortress has no fence to keep me from preying on the prey?

You wanting to play games and hide and go seek

But the rules to this game aren't fair, if someone already had a peek

Spare me the light, I worship in the dark

That's where my joy lies with you

Because when heaven's light is revealed, we're all going to burn

(2016)

PRESIDENTIAL COLLECTIONS

I started off with nothing, but a name and a dream

Went to school and college for a while, but they never spoke currency

Math was all x's and y's, but they never equaled to nickels and dimes

I wrote, read, studied, and tested on everything that was on paper, but none of it was printed on green

Graduated at the top of my class, but I had to learn my own way to make money, because the way I was taught in school never made any cents

From part time, to full time, to working two jobs, pennies turned into Lincolns that jumped on top of Benjamins

Bills were paid, mouths were fed, cars were gassed

But more money, more problems which us people should know

Used to water my garden of money, now it can barely grow

Accounts were full to perfection, but now are at an all-time low

Fighting for a change, I'll do anything to get my presidents back in my hands

A family on my shoulders, I'll support them at any cost

Squeezing pennies in my hands until they become nickels

Rubbing nickels until they became quarters

Praying on quarters until they became Andrew Jacksons

Buying to support until the next check comes in

Paycheck to paycheck life, it's weak to me like Monopoly play money

But soon enough the income will be eight figures rich

I want to walk with no balance because of the weight of my own money

To be injected with so much money, that my blood smells like fresh printed bills

And hold my money tighter than a money band

On the road to riches, money never comes as easy as it seems

No matter the flaws, I'm forever chasing the C.R.E.A.M.

(2016)

VERBALLY UNCONSCIOUS

Talking up a good talk that you wouldn't believe

But where's the contact if my eyes are bolted shut?

Body like a car, the mind built like an engine

But even in park, my engine is still on the go

Jarring up a storm I can't even hear, I guess it's intended for an unconscious audience

It's story time, but does the story make sense?

Is it all good or all bad? I hope it's not intense

A lot of people don't know how I think

I guess they'll have to wait until I'm asleep so they hear how I truly think

Am I crazy?

Am I exhausted? Am I insane?

To sleep out of restlessness while the brain is in pain

Words possibly taking on a life of their own, what verbal power do I control anymore?

The confidentiality is now a broken promise as I lay me down to sleep

To try to keep everything about me and my past out of the light

Just for it all to be spoken in the darkness of the night

Telling on myself there is no one else to take it out on

I am all I have; I am alone

Work is the best medication, and I'm scheduled for some overtime

Just to keep from sleeping

Overdosing until I crash, I am only repeating the cycle of late-night chatters

Waking up in a state of paralysis, feeling extracted, I am dead weight

In hope of a better tomorrow, I pray a treatment dreams its way to me

To cure me while I'm conscious so I can sleep properly when I'm unconscious

So, I can rest upon my pillow and know I'll have a good night's rest

(2016)

SHADE

Family, I am their provider

A guardian around demons, I am a soul survivor

But during my battles, I've found out during war who was really a friend and who was a foe

That some people I associate with talked behind my back

Confront them in person and words get muffled while their jaw stays locked

Even on the sunniest of days, shade is always being thrown

The king can never rule when someone is always trying to take his throne

I used to stay well connected, but now I choose to be alone

Seen me as a kid, or child, but I'm fully grown

Money, love, or business: take your pick

Time and energy are at an all-time low, so this needs to be quick

The family matters are strictly confidential

So, choose your questions carefully, because your expected answer will not show any credential

My old favorite snacks are starting to come back in my life

Because people always give me beef, and in the end, I'm the one labeled as a jerk

Life at work is never mellow, I'm normally prepared to strife

Long day, hard night, but can't sleep because people drive by on the lurk

Faith tested every day, because my body is in Holy War

You give me heat; I'll give you shade

You give me art; I'll give you truth

You give me life; I'll show you my world

And when you give me hell, I'll bring salvation

It may be a bright day, but the night will rise

It may be a sunny day, but the shade is partly cloudy

I hope you're ready for the storm when it's ready to strike

Because shade is like a broken condom, it provides no protection

(2016)

SHADE 2

Family, I am their provider

A guardian around demons, I am a soul survivor

But during my battles, I've found out during war who was a friend and who was foe

How signs were mistaken for signals

Driving down a dead end, I ended up making my own roads when I was surrounded with no material

Family is all about love and tradition that should be written in stone

Like a tombstone in a graveyard, it needs to be left alone

But there's always one who thinks they're superior; I should've known

They'd try to buy out their family and place themselves on top of the throne

In years past you surpassed sick, you had death on speed dial

The test of love and patience was my holy matrimony trial

The pain, finances, and the stress we endured; 'til this day you wouldn't believe

That everything was overtime, but we put in work as we rolled up our sleeves

Rental home, little income, but we gave you wealth

Medication and laughter, we nursed you back to health

Restored but not entirely, the treatment wasn't the same

A small household began to feud, and the fuse sparked a bad flame

A room per person, but we were all still divided

The arguing and fussing behind my back

Coming home with hate in the air, every second of breath felt so precious

So much sin and guilt that the fraction of our nuptials were close to being divided

Judgement was the new route, while communication was misguided

The winter rolled in, the snow was delayed, and for a while I was fine

Until a bone chilling scheme ran up my spine

My dream car only stayed in my dreams, because my transportation was limited with the situation I was in

I went to church for help, but nothing came about; maybe it was because church family couldn't share the same skin as I

Walking and biking to work, because money was my ultimate motive

Freezing rain, heavy snow, cold wind all kept me cool, while burning on the inside

Everything froze over except my pride

Because I know karma will go unnoticed, so I don't need to taste the revenge in the air

Too busy walking with blinders on, you'll never see the big picture

That your only purpose is to satisfy you and damn everybody else

The stress of you caused us not to see what was supposed to be delivered

Now we all had to die on the inside

I guess nine months was too much of a stretch

Those actions can never be forgiven

The road we were on together has reached a dead end

Only I can yield from here

Downing black coffee, I can see why your actions are so tasteless

You always preach a good sermon, but always revert back to sin

Outcast from my well beings, there is no coming back

(2016)

BRUTALITY

The past pain is just a decent memory

I don't have to be sanctified to know that I've been blessed

I don't need scriptures or be a hero with a cape to know that I've been saved

I use my talents and skills to help myself when my voice isn't enough

Nowadays logic equals violence

Lives are flat-lined

Race isn't measured in relays, but by skin

Red and blue lights flashing in our rear view too often

And cameras and videos are ready to film away

Day after day everybody purges and questions if 911 is the best answer to dial

Actions speaking louder than words, death becomes the exclamation point

Bullets flying more than birds and planes

Fists swinging more often than what's pay per viewed

Words and topics are exchanged faster than what's worth debating

Bodies dropping harder than quarterback sacks

Laughing at videos on the internet

It's all fun and games, but let a black body be lifeless on the ground

As the officer cuffs him and attempts to read him his rights

Will your perception change then?

If I try to preach black lives to the pigs, am I next to be bacon?

Already on the ground, and unarmed, and yet, they're still giving me a face full of pig feet

All lives matter, no one life should be taken by anybody

We try to preach this consistently, but is it being practiced?

The killings will stop when we learn to stop killing ourselves

After everything our ancestors fought for, I'm sure they wouldn't want us to go extinct

As we keep dropping, the government keeps collecting

The impact we need to have is more important than ever

Unity is something you can't subtract or divide

Only to add, increase, and gain

That's what the world needs

To heal and create true love and everlasting peace

(2016)

INSIDE MAN

Words were played off

Never expected it to evolve into action

The kitchen was the battlefield and it called for no ingredients

While you were preheating, I was already microwave hot

While you were offline, on standby, I became the bug that didn't need to fly to get the right information

I bypassed all the pass codes, so finger scans can't even lock me

And found out that your group was actually their group and you just got the invite

For years I been patient with jabs as we circled the ring

But now we're starting to reach the final round

Haymakers coming my way often

Inside and outside the ring, but I'm long overdue for connecting one

The aches, the bruises, the fractured bones, but you never seen me cry

The tears in my heart never showed on my face, so I never bled a drop

Scheming on a liar, the poker face players hide their final moves

On a continuation of forever, the things we never settle become a revolving door

But every in has an out and every entrance has an exit

I'm normally a gentleman, but I'm the only one leaving this merry-go-round

Driving your soul down straight when you could have taken a different path

The things you keep profiled away, will be worldwide webbed

Lying behind lies and laughter, only the lingering truth will lure you to liberty

But until then, the sands of time will continue to fall

When the sand is done, then my strike will be timeless

(2016)

FORWARD IN REVERSE

I never understood the logics of all things that are backwards

Because the things that are backwards to others, seems so straightforward to me

That doing something good can feel so wrong and sinning can feel so right

That every night I wake up, I brush my face and wash my teeth

And every morning I put on my pajamas to get ready for work

That when I begin driving in reverse on my way to the gas station, I make sure I fill it to E before I reach my next destination

That when the summer begins to get hotter, I start to get frostbite

So, when I get too cold, I simply turn on the air conditioner

When I get hungry, I eat a lot of water and when I get thirsty, I drink a lot food

Passing out from the itis, you would think I was fully conscious

My nightmare giving me peace, while my dreams gives me chills

Horror flicks make me laugh, while heartbreak stories give me trills

With all this knowledge, I tend to forget

As time moves slow, generations come quick

Children becoming parents, like that's any good

And more, and more we see misguidance being understood

The visual is so clear to the blind man's eyes, the sound is clearer to the deaf man's ears

That education today is mediocre

And fashion is the new fear

So, if a tree falls and no one is around, does it make a sound?

It's more like if the air didn't make a sound, and no one was around, did the tree really fall?

The disease of death is easy to catch, because life is uncatchable

The small blessings I claim, others take for a curse

What can I say? I just changed your whole forward perspective in reverse

(2016)

INCREDIBLE

You love me, I got you

I choose you, and hard trials, we flow through

Family man, country girl; I write art, you sing a tune

Taylor squad, but we're missing one; but it's okay, they're coming soon

Sagittarius of late November, and Gemini of early June

Two bodies trying to make one

Checking off hard trials, we deserve a reward, right?

Sacrificing us for them, as our love became limited

But united again, we adore every minute of every day

Gazing into those eyes, keeps my mind humble

The scents of me that you smell, keeps you secure

And the cuddles, they are always warm no matter the season

You hold me, love and kiss on me; with your cuteness, it's really unfair

With all those features and curves; thicker than an oak tree if I had to compare

If sex is the new drive, then I'm fueled up

Coming, soon to be the destination, then I'm on my way

Hit you from the back and give you whiplash, but call it an accident

Watch the airbags pop out from all my dents you couldn't prevent

Going through the battles of life

We win some, we lose some

We're happy, we're stressed

Money came and went

Friends come and go

But the loyalty we stand on, everybody else sat on

All our lives we had to fight

Piecing the puzzle of life together, we've learned how amazed it can be

We use our words and actions for protection without hoisting a gun

No need to race for your love when I already won

The love we share is incredible

Because I know I couldn't keep all this love to myself

(2016)

Evolving

As the world continues to change, so do I

Mind spinning like a hamster wheel, mind spinning like tires on the road

Words were lyrically spoken out of art, but now they are getting wise and bold

How things used to be obviously as the story was being told

Now it's all subliminal and hidden gestures you must behold

I keep a watch on my wrist because I lose track of time

Letting life age on me like fine wine

Waking up to the most high, because I know the sun is always going to shine

Bending over backwards for others, but my back has never broken

On the road to heaven, my mind took a detour to hell for its own heavenly sake

Came into this world clean, but life made me filthy

Oiled cross against my forehead a few times, baptized a few more times, prayed on my sins, all for another chance to be a Virgin Mary

Translating His words into my life, I then live it in art and write it in poetry

Make it into a book, but cherish it like my own diary

Childish at heart, mind is business savvy

The Gemini mind evolves every day; the inspiration to go on

And to make a better me, will always keep me happy

Turning the page of my mind bottled past, I cleared a new path

Dark clouds have cleared up, now I'm waiting on the rainbow to be the aftermath

I am half the man I used to be

The change I see deep inside of me, requires all four of my eyes to see

Because my mind wakes up on a 24-hour schedule

So, what I think has been presented for me, God's foreseen

Every day I make sure the next day I evolve

(2016)

BY MY SIDE

A dream that came to life, the imagination mixed with brainstorm caused God to allow you to rain down on me

I was young and I was thinking, but while I was thinking, I wasn't thinking about you

You came to me first; not too many women I've met came off as confident as you

You took me on a trip, mentally high over you, our relationship grew strong

Your figure is hard to put in words and trying to summarize your personality would take a thousand pages

Granted I've never seen you before, you've always followed me but never introduced yourself to me until now

No matter the case, I loved you instantly and allowed the years catch up eventually

Years went by, and time went by

Stress and life had me thinking less and in return, we went separate ways for a while

Money, school, work, and other girls had my life tangled up

All my temptation and pain in the air, it drove us further apart

Granted, you were always there, I stopped caring how you were and the feelings that came with it

But one day I came in touch with inner peace while listening to music and you came back

There was no sorry or apologies

We just picked up where we left off

Anger, love, happy, sad, frustration, sex, music, religion, peace, and emotions

We challenged them all

And never separated from any of them

There will be times where I just need space

And there will be times where I have other things to take care of before her

But she'll always be there

The bond being eternal, the love is forever

Despite all the pictures painted

Despite all the music being made

Despite all acting in plays

Despite all the scripts written

You'll always be the poetry that makes me a great poet

(2016)

WRITER'S BLOCK

What started off as unlimited, has worked its way to being limited

How ideas popped like popcorn to write, now are growing slow like vegetables in a garden

Like a pencil, as ideas were printed, the pencil slowly shrinks

I guess I was better off using a pen

The inspiration is slowly becoming a fading light

The motivation is repeatedly running into a wall like a crash test dummy

Maybe my vibe is off, maybe there is a bad smell in the air

I must need a new feeling to feel, or search for some roses to smell

The love I have for writing is out in the desert drying out, when I need it to flow like a river

Mentally, I need a reality check

Or do I need my brain washed, so I can be hypnotized into consistent work?

The passion is there, but the thought process is currently on a detour

The goals I have in mind for this art are reaching their final mark

This hobby I admired is running out of gas and there's no pump station in sight

Where do I go from here?

I still have so much to say but can't seem to get it out

Is it time to move on?

I fight myself to ignore the potholes and speedbumps, but I think my charisma has flat tires

All signs are meant to be read

As much as I try to ignore my own, it might be time to catch up on some reading

My art is dying

And right now, it's hard to keep it alive

Hopefully these words don't take life, I need to write

So, write I must

Because I still have so much to say and write

(2016)

PRIMETIME

I've entered that phase

When no one can touch me

When you feel unstoppable, knowing there is an unmovable object just waiting to slow you down

But like a mattress, I'm often slept on

With all these rappers and underground artists, I guess I'm under them

That's fine, that only means I'm closer to the core

Touch me if you want, and see how hot I can really get

Often at times, I treat my brain like a lighter

My ideas and creations are fire

Despite the fact I might burn myself in the process

The truth is often art, so the burn is just a reminder

So, to the ones that love to doubt, may you feel this to the third degree

Burning their doubts and given them my glasses so they can better see

So, when they see my success, that lightspeed is trying to keep up with me

So, when others claim I'm wasting time, I'm trying to make more

And the friends I used to have, were better off as enemies

I'm trying to stay at the same pace with the universe, my down time must always stay up

My time is here, my confidence is overqualified

My prime is now, I'm as rare and as raw as it comes

(2011)

HER SKIN

If I was forever blind to this world, her body would be the needed prescription to see always

Thin where she likes it and thick where she wants to be, I see how we interact without even being in motion

But her skin

Her skin does something to me

The lightest gentle touch and my stimulation warms up rapidly

I allow her to run her hands through my hair just so my mind can remember what comfort and compassion can do to me

As she reveals herself, I can see every curve and every kissable tattoo as a minor glow appears

Asking to be held, I can feel it all

Rubbing and massaging her all over, the oil made her brown skin a golden glow

Holding one another and locking lips, the moist smoothness of her lips could heal any chapped lips

Letting her rub her hands down my back, I cling to her tight, as goosebumps begin to spring

Feeling her tears fall on me, but her eyes form no tears

Introduce myself into her soul so we can both bask in the same glow

Skin friction, back scratches, and handprints

The two rubbed and lit like matches

The fire being made could brighten the darkest corner of every room

While my body looks as though it just came from a street brawl, you remain golden like a trophy

I guess I can say I'm the first-place winner

It's true time heals all wounds

But the way you attacked me, I'll allow these wounds to scar up so your signature remains forever

(2017)

PAGES

Today's love will never be the same as it was yesterday

Yesterday's memories will never be the same as they are right now

As you countlessly remind me how much my mistakes bother you

And some nights you are restlessly awake or cry yourself to sleep

You think I'm careless, or I have a shallow soul, but I am a defensive emotional human being

Your pain is my pain; if you're cut, I'm the one who bleeds

Though I may never show it

Through all the emotional roller coasters, door slamming, and arguments

I still and will always love you

And have you smiling and laughing as often as possible

I love being locked into your eyes, while wrapping you into my arms

To be the light to your dark stormy nights

To be both sword and shield to this corrupt world

To be the tissue to wipe away whatever tear that may fall

I know you have so many fears and concerns; that you doubt

But I made an oath to make you that I shall proclaim; even if it takes a lifetime

As our final chapters close, a new one will soon open

As future parents, we will have so much to teach and show our soon to be daughter

As we wander off in her eyes and smile, we'll know we will be able to handle it all

Everything will be fine

I promise I will protect us as we all learn, love, and grow as a family

I love you as a best friend, a wife, and now a soon to be mom

Our chapter may be coming to an end, but our story is endless

I want our book to grow with pages upon pages of everything

If we have each other, and love, then every day will be a page worth of unconditional love

(2017)

REKINDLE

Dead inside

His bones are cracking into dust as my heart grows stony

He walks these shallow grounds soulless while his veins thirst for blood

Can a simple prayer restore this dead corpse?

Because these feelings are now smoky from a burning fire of love and youth that's been put out

Stumbling into beauty, she looks past his present state

Her hands are warm to the touch as he begins to heal his dead, pale, cracked skin

Her lips were soft against his which streamed blood flow into him again

She holds him, and make him inhale her aroma as her warm embrace restores his current diminished soul

The fire that once laid in a bed of smoke and dead wood is rekindled

His skin is healing, heart is pumping

His youth is restored!

Did she become the prayer I never asked for?

Staring into her lovely eyes, he sees desire in her eyes

He then takes her by the hand

Kisses her with gentle kisses on the neck

As he slowly inches closer to her ear, he says, "I'll reward you with all of me, if it's worth living for"

As she bites her lips, he gave her something to die for

(2017)

RICH MINDED

Not everything about me is shiny like gold

And sometimes I get cut by diamonds

You can never see me selling my soul for soulless cash

Because I'm forever rich minded

Bedazzled by the false sense of reality

The cheapness we often experience will rust or break apart

Everybody wants to aim for diamonds and pearls

But often must settle with bronze and rhinestones

As rose gold as she is

She can only be promised silver and pearls

Never disappointed, because she never allowed jewels to rob her of her self-beauty

Rings and necklaces never meant a thing, when you have a real ruby jewel in between your chest

The chrome on my shoulders will always help my ruby shine

No price, bargain, or clearance can buy that

Blinded by materials, when the real jewels have been

ourselves all this time

So why buy yourself, when you've always been free?

Keep shinning, you're priceless

(2017)

AVA'S EYES

When I close my eyes, I see your eyes

Because right now, we cannot see eye to eye

Months apart, but Father Time is counting down

'til the day I can look you in the eyes

To be the first man you gaze upon

To cry, laugh, drool upon; and even pull on my hair

To put all your strength onto holding my finger, and give me that title of "Daddy"

The day I hold you would be like holding the world in my hands

And with every waking day, presents a new adventure

Not every day will be sunny; often I'll have to face gloomy days

But just like the sun, I'll promise you the day will never end without you shinning at least once

Even if I must fight the clouds

Give me your eyes

The watery eyes, the sleepy eyes, the angry eyes, and even the tired eyes

That's all I desire

Even if I was stripped of all other senses, I only would want to keep my eyesight just to see you daily

The emotions I used to lack will be born upon your arrival

How many times will my heart melt? Only God knows

Because you would be a blessing to me and a possible cure to the many things I may not know are coming my way

Locked in some of my ways

Can you be the key to unlocking my many doors?

Can you redefine me when I assumed I was insolvable?

What can I say?

If I'm the guitar, you would be the string to daddy's heart that causes me to tune

No matter what face I present, I see that you see right through me

You can tell by my eyes

It's obvious that I love you even if you're not here yet

But we're both due very soon

For you to see me

And for me to see you and say I love you

So, you know the voice you've heard from the other side is true

Through my eyes, you'll always see that I love you

(2017)

M

M, Marissa

A marvelous mother in the making

A mommy to be

A miraculous maiden in the beginning, to a married mistress

A well-mannered male as I, managed to measure out one another's love

My mission is to never mislead, to add and not divide; so, math those mathematics

To manage all problems with minimum effort

And maybe get my master's degree to show the world I've studied in all things Marissa

But the mutual love we have is worth maintaining

There's no mystery that this is for you

Like the sun rising in the morning, the mighty God has blessed you with another magnificent day

But this May I might have to call mayday for this Mother's Day

Because Mrs. Marissa will be a mommy

And I'm not sure how much my mind can mass or measure this moment

M,

It might be the thirteenth letter in the alphabet, but you're always first to me

It doesn't take a manual or magazine to read how much I love you

So, no matter how messy, mediocre, or mean we may be

Our love for one another erases all margins of error

I love you, Marissa

Happy Mother's Day

(2017)

A FANTASY TEASE

The friendliness of a friendship became unexplained

Misguided paths and foreseeing the unpredictable sparked a mysterious fantasy

How friends intertwine a unique bond

Sharing the same qualities, generated a one-sided fixation for the other

How his mind boiled a toxic lust and desire

The many desirable questions of her looks, featured figures, skin, and how tasty her edibles could be

Knowing that they are true in the most friendliness of bonds, it will not surpass that line

The ultimate tease as the friend status stays mutual

During the night, a dark stormy clouded mind is raining temptation as he hungers for her

As thunder echoes what could be her moans and the bed squeaking

The lightning streaks across his brain, which causes him to talk in his sleep

The filth he utters while his eyes are bolted shut

The dream he foresees is only a tease for what doesn't exist

Waking up with a pounding heart and moist skin, you'd think the dream was real

And yet, he just wakes up alone

Everything felt like a one-night stand that never really existed

He sees you and he wants you, but he can't have you, as he sees and talks to you daily

It feels like he's under a spell or drug; this sorcery fix can't be real

Confined to his own personal ways, he can never physically show you how he truly feels

(2017)

GOOD MORNING MOON

3am

I rose and set like the sun

I'm now in competition to watch the moon set before I do

I've battled the trials of the day, and yet I lay here restless

Am I a wolf?

Must I howl so you can set?

Can you provide me a solution to my restlessness?

Must I prowl and hunt through the darkness of the morning to seek my rest?

I want to sleep, that's where my peace lies at

A resort of dreams where trials are nonexistent

Where life becomes a fantasy of my choosing with no consequences or punishments because of my choices

A relief like vacation for seven to eight hours before another series of trials confront me as the day begins to unfold

What does tomorrow truly bring if my restlessness always confronts the moon?

While the sun burns my eyes, I am presented no shade

The moon cools me while shining in the darkness of the night

I am condemned to stare with no promise of rest

As the journey of restlessness continues, my bed's comfort remains anonymous in search of a good night's rest

This mission seems impossible to complete

(2017)

THE FATHER IN ME

You,

You are the most beautiful un-birthed piece of art no one has yet to see

The greatest wait I could ever wait for

The future of me, through your own eyes

All those empty voids, all these dark empty spaces would brighten and flood over upon the first cry I hear; upon the tears you've placed on me

Place yourself on me

As you wrap your hand around my finger, you get a little peek of my world; but you're my favorite planet

So, it's safe to say we alone form our own universe, as our love bursts into countless stars

I could never see myself leaving you, because it would be hard to say goodbye

As each day you get older, yesterdays can only be formed as memories I can no longer relive

I guess you can say I'll be Father Time, just to value every moment together

And your mom will Mother Nature you our world of countless adventure

And as we revolve around you and all your greatness, I would assume you'll be our personal plant that's out of this world

My first, like the number one

My beginning like A in the alphabet

My heart which allows me to live and protect

My joy to brighten my life and humor all that surrounds you

I've done a lot of growing up to be at this point in my life; to be a father,

To have a daughter, to help hearten a dad of rebellious remorse will be the greatest story to unfold right in front of me

When you finally confront me

You will be a dream worth waking up to repeatedly

But until then, sleep and kick away inside

For when you arrive, the fight to hold these love-filled tears

This will be an eye-opening experience for everyone to see

Even for me

The unconditional tears of fatherhood

(2017)

TOT'S HEART

You are my heart, forever your keeper

You flow through me like blood, and grow on me like hair on my head

You cause me to beat each second you cross my mind

And thump when I often forget to include you in my day

As you grow, I grow

When you're hurt, I ache

I simply want you to wake up and live every day like a dream

Where fantasies are kept, and love is an unbroken shielded promise

Hear me, listen to me

Know that my words are weapons of protection and comfort to strengthen you

To someday make my innocent princess into a phenomenal queen

Reveal the curses and shadows of the world and give us all your lighted aroma

Let every cry, yawn, hiccup and laugh change our world forever

You are the ultimate pulse that makes me go

I feel the love, I feel your love

Because seeing you every day would make me forget tomorrow ever existed

I'm holding on to you for dear life for as long as I can

For when it's time for me to finally let go, I'll have a hard time keeping you all to myself

But no matter what roads and challenges of life are presented to you, I'll always be present

And pass down the knowledge to help you pass at life, always

(2017)

REBELLIOUS REBEL

If you're looking for love, well in its heart you'll find trouble

Where luck implodes like bombs, and your dreams are stripped like a football fumble

My action speaks volumes, while your words only choke and muffle

Because this is my uprising of a quietly unknown rebellious rebel

Your way isn't my way

Because when I make some ways, you consider them no way

So, some paths we make are either dead ends or fork roads

Often like friendships, we end here or move on

My story has no title, but people often try to give me names

To judge and critique and not applaud what I overcame

How some try to guide when they can't really lead

So, in the end I proceed to protect what I love and what I breed

So, if I cut new or old ties, there's no need to bandage it; let it bleed

And know that time will heal all wounds with God speed

Life has no manual, so what are you trying to understand

You're better off creating a new milestone instead of surpassing what used to be

Granted I am young, I'm close to introducing a youngster to my world

But I plan to define my own meaning

Not add to the statistics of my generation

To change through action, because voices can't be viewed

So, watch how the close critics see how I grew to be a flame lily, when everybody expected another dandelion weed

So, to all my doubters

To all the people that may judge and hate on me

Just know my erect is direct

So, when you think my come up is late

Just know I'll always comes when the time is right

So, when you're expecting a ringer, just know I'm a knocker

That cardiac arrest came about because I am a heart stopper

The educated language and etiquette attire were always bound to have me improper

While some people prefer me to pretend to shine like silver; when their attitude is dull like penny copper

My war is hot because the peace, my inner peace, is becoming so cold

Rebel, rebel, rebel all day long; where it provides protection around my soul

(2017)

H.O.E (HELL ON EARTH)

An eternal life of fighting and survival may soon be coming to an end

She's trying

She's making changes for all lives, but it's never good enough

The mother that once nurtured us, is dying

I mean damn, with so much smoke and pollution in the air, no wonder she has us trapped in a green house

Spring feeling like a dry summer's eve

While winter is always in the fall as we reminisce of what snow used to be

Drilling her so much, we can't tell if it's helping or hurting her

Planting seeds in her to watch the sprouts grow big and tall and eventually leave like leaves blowing in the wind

While other times we plant dead seeds that even daisies can't grow over

In the end, her legs and her emotions can't stop quaking

As animals question the logics of survival, we have become what animals used to be

Killing and hurting each other like it's as normal as breathing

Killing off humanity, I guess she must die with us

To no longer choke on the lies of unanswered change

And cough up the truth and tear over a new generation

We would look at it as if it was an apocalypse, but she knows its Judgement Day

They are just two of the same

We spit, throw trash, and urinate all over you

Despite the love you give to yourself and us, we only see you as a source when you help give us a reason to live and breathe

Medicines, cures, plants, and food

All these things you give

But others see drugs, sex, money, and war

This is indeed hell on earth

Because no matter how much she is used or loved upon, she'll always be there

To always help us even when we don't give thanks in return

I guess we're all pimps

Because while some see her as the greatest mother of all

There are many to see her as the biggest hoe to have never died

(2017)

JABS

They are preaching on my name, knowing they have no religion behind it

So, practice your lines before you attempt to practice what you preach

They forget the family has more than two eyes

They forget the family has more than two ears

Not taken on the role of God, but I see and hear all that surrounds us

You are moving solo, while we move in packs

So, when you try to attack one, you're trying to attack us all

You'll fail every time, we move in pride

Our house is a humble home

While some are in search of a house while still living in a discarded home

Inside the ring, some have blinded us

Haymakers of no contact and arguments; what a disconnect

I mean damn, we graduated from vows to parenthood, where is the applause at?

But that's okay

The gloves are coming off as I circle them with jabs

But when the forgiveness comes is when the haymaker reconnects

No need to count, just stay down

Ding, ding, ding

(2017)

THESE EYES SO FAR

These eyes so far

Twenty-four years' worth of history viewed

But humbly blessed for the lens I see out of; to help separate the vision between you and I

Because some can't view a liar even if they were blind

As much as the body and mind can be a professional liar, only the eyes speak the truth

As much as I try to keep my blinders on the goals in mind, the hate and negativity often catches the side eye

As I see and witness family fill the earth

The memories run down my face so heavy even my eyelids couldn't catch them all

As I pray with my eyes wide shut, the darkness I encounter will draw me closer to the light

So, when God begins to give me visions of my dreams, I approach them with no sleep intended

To work and support until my eyes are red and tired

To see a better vision for the legacy I will one day leave behind

Because despite never going to Paris or seeing the Eiffel

The legacy I'm leaving behind is as beautiful as Paris, and she's worth an eyeful

As I reread my old poems

I see how direct I used to be

But now, I'm writing more exclusive and subliminal as I now see what others don't

To protect what I create, to protect what I birthed that caught my eyes

Sometimes art requires you to see without seeing

To test your sight in the dark, to generate the brightest creations

And yet while I continue to keep my eyes laser focused, I feel like my best work has yet to shine

When I'm finally blinded by the awakening of you

My vison will forever be 20/20 clear

(2017)

REMINISCING WITH SEDUCTION

Reversing the sands of time

Blowing dust off the chest of memories past

And there was when I spotted you again

The lustful desires of compassion had us focus driven at one point

Times we were apart felt like years compared to hours

And the time together will forever be unforgettable

Time drew us together

The joy of companying each other

The laughs, the kisses, and the sex

The dates, the drives, and the phone calls had left us addicted

The itch to find time together even if it was just merely seconds

The shakes and chills when our bodies touched

The aroma we inhaled from one another stimulating all our senses

So how can we walk away from all this?

Our double lives are what kept our thrill alive, so why put

what we loved on life support?

Was this meant to die?

Time

Time made us castaway

But time does allow things to repeat

So, can we reunite?

Or is it all just a waste?

Are we losing our minds, or are we allowing our minds to lose us?

I ponder these things for twenty-four hours

Pondering about you, with no sleep intended

Because the best sleep I'll ever get is by sleeping with you

So, is this love, or simply for the love of the moment?

We flirted with danger many times before

Is it possible to do it all over again?

To hold you once again

To feel you and kiss you

To long for what used to be

Because through our eyes, all we see is satisfaction and seduction

To feed what can't get full

A trill in slumber that needs awakening once more

A desirable pleasure only one can obtain

Do you remember these things such as I?

Let's re-enact the past in modern day time

(2017)

FULSOME LIGHT

I asked her one day if she loved me despite my light

I mean, I know I'm not as loud as thunder or as flashy as lightning

So, is my love a guiding light?

She told me she's loved me since I was just a spark that barely had a flame to my name

Despite how bright or dim I saw myself, she only cared for my light that was there

Because, when she was often alone in the dark, I became the nightlight that shined her fears away

And granted I'm not the brightest light bulb in the box or as hot or bright as the sun, but she never let me go dark or overheat

She captured me with her crazy colored neon lights

Never dim, always bright

But the pain was never seen until we looked through the x-ray light

So, the brightest she compelled couldn't shine in the night

Not even her high beams could help her face the darkness that was ahead

But along came this shining star

This little flame of no name that became her tunnel light

I brightened her prospective

I shined when it was most needed

Stronger together, we captured heaven's light, with no batteries needed

Now, we have our own shining star we must brighten

So, one day she can be the path to one day help someone that is blinded by the darkness

And to continue the light we passed on

Try to fill and surround this family in darkness and watch how we shine

The brightness we put out will cause everyone to see

No path of darkness will be an easy one

But when it's over, every path will be lit

(2017)

HER REST

The best thing about me is you

Giving me the title of fatherhood is no easy task

But your warm embracing smile makes it all worth it

And when you're at rest, you create eternal peace

Are you dreaming about you?

Are you dreaming about me?

Are you dreaming about your family?

Do you treat every dream like your first debut?

Are they nightmare free?

Everything you do in your sleep is an endless possibility

As the moonlight shines upon your face

And the clouds drift you upon the night sky, may the counting sheep keep you in slumber

For when the sun shines, a new journey and adventure will be waiting on you

Until that first yawn comes as the day turns into night

As the moon reappears while you're at rest

(2017)

NORMALITY

What is normal?

What makes you normal?

Is my normal different from your normal?

Does it make us weird?

Our livelihood is separated by life itself

We can't all walk the same line

Each road leads to a different sign

Some right-handed people can't write with their left, while some lefties can't write with their right

Where are the rules that establish what is solidified as normal?

Because obviously I've never read them

What I do I consider it to be normal

While some may label me as crazy or abnormal, they be odd themselves for not living the same as I

Judgement is born out of things that can't seem to be understood or agreed upon

Compromising is only a temporary treaty

Normal is something that truly can't be explained

No language, skin, or culture can provide a solution

So in the end, we try to express our normal to others

Only to create racism, war, and chaos amongst the planet

Normal

It's so normal to say, but is lived differently amongst the world

We're all wired in our own normal way

No one way is the right way

So as normal as you are, you're still weird in the end

(2017)

SENSELESS

I know I'm not sleeping, because you're a dream come true

You have me feeling like a hammer in a toolbox, because I want to nail you

Your lustful desires and curious adventures have left me defenseless

Using me for all I'm worth has left me vulnerable and senseless

The way you make me feel is nothing less than spectacular

Loads of fun and full of energy

No drama intended; no headaches provoked

But when we're alone, you know what to give me when the aches aren't provoked

That then causes me to tear up while my eyes remain dry

Not every touch is stimulating, but you often know how to feel me up

From hand holding to handcuffs, from massages to scratches

You innocently have gifted hands, but aggressively have the Midas touch

What I desire to taste requires no utensils or hands

My taste buds require a taste that can't be grown, manufactured, or processed

It's a fulfilling edible that can never fill me up

Served one way only, I can never get enough of what you got

To ingest what you produce, to intake what you give out

You're shaped to amaze, I love the way you workout

Let's do a session together, so we can see if our stamina can handle a few burnouts

From opera to singing, your vocals are well

But behind closed doors can sound like muffed moans, so who can tell?

That less can be more, and more can be less

While other's ears can hear sounds of pleasures or violet distress

Whether we're in tune or simply conversing, these ears are always here to hear

To make sure the outside noise is dead, so you'll always be crystal clear

So when you say my name repeatedly in exhaustion, it'll ring in my ear

Her sounds are music to my ears

No hearing aid can misconceive

Her presence doesn't have to be far to inhale her aroma

No perfume needed, her presence is lavender

Her mornings are Japanese cherry blossoms and her nights are moonlight pleasures

Being with you daily is like being in a store full of candles

Every day is a different aroma

The fire and passion we'll make will ignite the room into a storm of fragrance

Winter will never be around if you remain a spring breeze

And when things get hot, I'll never go nose blind to your summer's eve

I can always see you, but be blinded by your presence

To see you daily is well beyond all the other senses

To see you express as you express with me

Blurry to the world's sin, you correct my vision to see a better portrait of the universe's art

Granted, your facial expressions and kinky desire in your eyes are fascinating, I just love seeing you just because

So, do my eyes really blink?

Yes, but only when you're away

Because when I'm with you, I want to capture everything together

(2018)

LIFETIME

Time, it's a never-ending process

The test of time is a test everyone is destined to fail

Whether it be wasted time or having a good time, time has never lost to no being

So, when it comes to my time, I watch it

I spend a lot of money to make my wrist heavy, so I can keep up with time, but never waste it

I can never let a minute go by without counting the seconds

But in case I miss something, I'll always have a watch watching my watch

Watching time so long, our conversations are starting to tick tock

While you ring by the hour, my body is categorized as an alarm

Watching you 24/7, my eyes get red, but my body never snoozes

Blinking by the second, can you count them up by the hour?

I want you to watch me as I watch you watch me see you lose track of time

To claim me as victor and possibly story this moment in a once upon a time

That I've battled against time and won

That I didn't have to reverse time to timely figure out how to out-do you at your own craft

But realistically, time is always changing

Watching you 'til the end of my time would be a waste of my own

Trying to compete with time is a challenge no one is willing to waste

I guess now I can dream big elsewhere on my spare time

(2018)

MONEY HEREAFTER

Money come, money go

People come, people go

They ask for help, so here I go

But return the help? They a no show

Call 'em up about the dough

Arguments rise, they cut me so

But through it all, I'm still me though

Because people come and people go

Money come and money go

But my money will come, and my money will flow

In case some people already didn't know

(2018)

NIGHT PROWL

Sin dances in the nighttime

Like a cold crisp breeze under a full moon

I seem to blow my way into her mind

I whispered past her fears to give her some excitement

I gave her mind an unexplained feeling

As those words became action, I gave her a reason to like these changes

That they became a consistent sensation every night

That she's willing to wait all day to dance in the nighttime

Only wanting to sleep the day away, I alone can keep her awake during the night

Giving me all her time, energy and youth, that the daytime can't manage to sober her

I've become that fix that keeps her high

That what she supplies me never dries out like the night is long

If we stay in the shadows of the night, no one else could see

Because the light provides punishment

We'll keep ourselves from the truth if deception keeps us satisfied

That lust fills the night air as dancing becomes a midnight pleasure

Humans by day, animals at night

If I eat it raw, I'm serving it raw, there's no need to season it with flavors of protection

We're just animals that love to prowl in the night

Dancing under a full moon

The beastie animal within seductively engaged in the cold breeze of the night

(2018)

THE TRANSPARENCY

Exposure wasn't supposed to be the aftermath for the games I've played

But when you create rules as you play, others will see you only played yourself

So now the fallback game is strong

My roots are exposed that dirt no longer wanted to cover; I guess someone was digging me

Blinded by karma, she wasn't feeling me

But whatever the case may be, I'm in court fighting for love so these vows won't separate or be considered maybes

That maybe we can let the past remain in its name and pray the future is no more pain

Close to losing it all, I can only gain

I can admit the things I did were insane

That hurting you to better my love was okay in my brain

Now I can't buy the things that make you happy, because time has no price

Water in my eyes, they never flow

Sadness in my heart, but never aches

Ego and pride molded me, but love is a fighting mustard seed

The growth is slow but promising

The burnt foundation will be greener on the other side

The first aid, nurse, and protector I was supposed to be was none of the above

The multiple tests I was given for multiple chances, I kept cheating

Wanting to be so incredible and invincible, that I forget that I still bleed too

That I can see what she sees, but can't seem to feel that way too

Praying for answers that I've questioned

Putting in the work to restore my faith, I only want to level things out to peace and love

Once I viewed the darkness, now blinded by the light

Because I must see that there are brighter days ahead

Driving for your love, the exit is many miles ahead

But my route and pace will be steady

Because once I reach that destination, I'll never past it again

(2018)

EVERYTHING IS LOVE

Everything is love, everything was love

A young couple in puppy love

Saw it in each other's eyes they wanted forever love

That fun love, that good love, that made everything all love

Claimed it in their vows, so each love became one love

As they began a new path of unconditional love

The love was strong, the love was right

That they ended up making love

Small challenges and trials came and went to divide their love

But all failed; they had strong love

But too many times his love wasn't her love

That the challenges of life that was passable, passed into self-love

Which made unconditional love into weak love

Seeking on sin, the love he found was the wrong love

The trill of sinful love made him abandon real love

Caught in the act, he gets no love

Drama is an all-time high, as he battles family love

Thinking in her head, "How could you hurt love?"

But through all the pain, there is still love

As they seek holy love to rebuild love

So, everything can be back at happy love

Because as much hurt as the world offers, they are thankful for love

Everything is love, everything is love

Unity in love is always the right love

(2018)

LOVE FOR GENERATIONS

Love is the final piece to the puzzle

Love is unconditional

Love lights the path to the person you were meant to be with

For better and for worse

Love is a story that can be told to multiple people in multiple ways

From generation to generation

The action may be different, but wording of the message is still the same

I love you

(2015)

THE MOTIONS

How can I catch a break when the break is uncatchable?

I mash the pedal, but life just keeps on going

Life has so many speeds, I can never require a brake

That people suck at being fast, that it's slowing me down

But when I finally catch speed, I'm clocked by cameras

Money came and went in a flash

I guess I couldn't see the bigger picture

Hate dreaming slow

Because now I must drive fast

All these miles must add up to something

Racing against time, will the finish line be my success?

On the road to many roads, which part is set for me?

No destination is the final destination; the road map has me following my trails to destiny

I'm sure she's fine, but success hasn't always been

Used to think love was all speed bumps and potholes

Red lights and stop signs couldn't stop me at max speed

But one came along and made me raise my E-brake

It was hard to slow down at the time, but when I was able to stop, her attraction created the traction that left my wheels smoking

Steamier than a roaring engine, you left my drive for your love in neutral

Slow motion is better than no motion

Detailing the depths of you took notion

You began to read me like a manual as your fuel ignition some emotion

I never thought this could be real

Me telling you know I feel

Now she's in my driver's seat, meshing the pedal and palming the wheel

Now she drives me crazy, but I know I really like it

She jacked me up, fixed my flats, and now I'm racing to her love

So we can Sunday drive all these miles together

No matter the storm or any weather

I'm willing to slip, slide and skid together if it means we're forever bumper to bumper

(2018)

EDIBLE FOREPLAY

For the longest time, I've been watching you and reading you like a menu

Wanting to skip past appetizers and entrees, I only have a sweet tooth for dessert

So, can I sink my teeth in you?

To see what flavors I manage to taste

To have it linger around, even after the aftertaste

Are your cakes soft like cotton?

Is your pie as creamy as banana cream?

If I managed to fork you off a plate, am I promised to taste all of you?

To be able to eat all of you with no evidence of crumbs

Devouring you down like a fat kid eating birthday cake

Blowing your back, mind, and soul, like fire to a candle

Pleasuring the sweetest of the sweets, you leave me icier than the tallest wedding cake

It's easy to describe you as ice cream

But if you're the ice cream, can I be your ice cream cone?

So, in case you drip, it can run on me

Or do you prefer to be in a bowl?

Whereas though I can serve you this banana, cover you in fudge until it drives you nuts

Will that be the cause to make your cherry pop? Or are you simply caramelized?

Either way you try to scoop it, every day can be our special sundae

Even if that sundae happened on a Sunday

I just want to lick, eat, and repeat until I get frostbite

Every sticky situation must always be a delicious one

Me and you go well together like cookies 'n cream

And with so much heat coming from your oven, I'm surprised there's no bun in it yet

But regardless of the time or day, I'll always make room for dessert

So how much are you willing to serve me for this tip?

I just hope you can handle my sweet tooth

Because my stomach can never be full from the sweets you dish out

(2018)

YEARS AHEAD

Thinking, plotting, scheming years ahead of me

Wanting, fighting, chasing for a chance to create a future so far ahead of me

That I hurt, sin, bleed and sacrifice for a chance to see a better me

But if I cried years from now, how would that manage to affect the present me?

Daydreaming on the what if's in life

Working to birth these dreams like the birth of a family

Seeing my children grow and run, despite them not being with me daily

A father to only two, the what if's will forever remain for the ones whose stories never took chapter

As mind-boggling as things may be, time presents no pause

Every day presents the future

But the future, I envision, is far beyond what the next day reveals

Caught between space and time, my mind is galaxies away from me

From parenthood at its finest, to career paths attached to a loving family home, to seeing my elderly days

My vision often separates me from reality and operates on fantasy

Years from now, on a day I once called someday, love will be restored

That tomorrow becomes today, and I no longer present love with pain

And that temporary unconditional theme becomes a promise for a lifetime

Years ahead on where I want to be, versus where time has me now; only to still remain behind

Time watching for the future, waiting for that time to presents itself, so I can no longer envision the future, now that it's here

To wake up from these dreams and live the future I've been given

So, the tomorrows I used to envision and think about, I'll be prepared for me

(2018)

BLIND EYE MURDER

Do you want to be a witness to something you've never seen?

Where decisions result in murder

Generations of "what could be" and "what if's"

And those dreams were never given to the ones that never slumbered

Within this life, I offer new life

But within this life of new life, I've become a witness to something I couldn't see

And it's only because I allowed love to be a multitude of titles

When it was never a love story to begin

Like a soldier in the army, I fight wars to keep the peace

But the peace within me couldn't settle the war on my outer image

As my peace dies a little every day, my heart beats and pulses for the unknown I became a witness to

I guess some peace had to be aborted, like a mission, to settle some wars

As peace is restored

A father with his head beyond the clouds, my mind is wider than space

Looking to be a five-star dad, I've only been rated a two

Looking light years beyond my space, I want these stars to shoot to infinity

So the fulfillment of their dreams satisfies me for the other dreams I didn't allow to even slumber

For I witnessed murder my eyes couldn't see

(2018)

TALK 'N TEXT

She likes him and he wants her, so they talked about it

But the public has microphones for ears, so they texted about it

Building bonds through work, that's how they worked around it

Playing on words and subliminal gestures is how they sexted about it

The attention she was giving, he paid that

Everything was like a mutual game, they both played that

He's bending over backwards just to get some play in that

But she's already bent over; he couldn't imagine that

Phone starts buzzing, now he can picture that

Now if he sees this in real life, could he really feel that?

But they're both living life on the double, so they understood that

The sex life she talked about, he liked about her

The pictures weren't just because, he had to make her

The aggression and domination were a turn on, that's what pleased her

The gestures and skills he downplayed were what teased her

So, when words become action, he'll make her into a believer

So, that when she sees him punch in, he'll be ready to work her

The way he looks at her, she knew something special would come out of him

Bonding often, she found they have a lot in common, which made her really like him

Necessarily didn't have to trip to fall for him

Never gone too long or else she'll miss him

She watched him sponge up all the info she leaked him

Now it's time to dish out, is she willing to clean him?

All party play, no strings attached, but this subliminal game has her attached to him

If he doesn't hear from her during the day, then he's texting her

When she needs to vent and the coast is clear, then she's calling him

Not friends, not partners, not close associates, but all the above; and that's that

The game and rules they play by no one else can understand; that's how you go discreet about it

(2018)

FAMILY COME UP

Oh man, oh man

These kids, these kids

When one is asleep, the other is awake

When one is talking, the other is crying

When one is feeding, the other is playing

Imbalance work hours with family time, sleep is rare to come by

So how can I manage time, when I can't even juggle it?

But even with my hands tied behind my back, don't expect me to shake hands for too many helpful handouts

Burped on, crawled on, even farted on

Hair pulled, sneezed on, and poked at

Diaper changes are the danger zone

Because when pee shoots, there is no safe zone

Whether playing games or on the phone, there's not enough free time to be left alone

But working so much, the time I get, I cherish more and more

The teachings and tickles often bring me joy

As daddy rings in my ear from their squeaky voices, it reminds me that they'll always need me

As a father, a provider, a protector, and perhaps even a hero

I always envisioned and dreamed before and after parenthood

Now as a family man, I only want to give them the world, when I once thought it was all mine

The road I stress and fight to create, will help them drive to success on the same path I once walked

Oh man, oh man,

These kids, these kids

You've got to love these wild, crazy, adventurous kids

(2018)

SPECIAL DELIVERY

In order to play hero, you must be equipped for battle

You entered a fortress of the unexpected, and made friends with a snake

Your remarks label you as an asshole, but your actions are too timid to back it up

I know only God can judge, but I'm a hell raiser

Karma is your demise, I am its deliverer

The sin you seek is the punishment you'll reap

The vows you honored haven't progressed forward

You've been exposed for the double life, and yet, you're the only one that don't know

Wifey has changed to better help you, but you keep following the night

No matter what mask you hide behind, I know your identity

I'm just trying to be real with you

I gave you life lessons

I gave you views in which you never saw

But as you obtained, you let go too

In one ear and out the other, I've wasted my time while feeling disrespected

Now I silence my help for you, while remaining cool

But I remain true to the things you blind yourself by

Letting beauty go unnoticed, she tries her hand

So, while you're on the clock, someone else is punching in on her time

So, the time you've earned, that new person is getting for free

Boy, you just don't get it

I'm all up in your house

I'm in your kitchen clicking like a stove

Let the fire ignite so I can keep cooking up the things you think I don't know

That's she's always the aggressor because you won't show these things when she challenges your manhood

So egotistic and have so much ammunition about her past

But if you can't heal from the things you won't reveal, then I guess I'll be the asshole who will assist you unexpectedly

But as cool as we are, you are exposed

I'd just wish you were more aware

I only want the best for everyone; including you

But damn, you must be more understanding

Only then the man you are destined to be will be able to stand

(2019)

DAY IN A LIFE: ZELDA

Close your eyes

Then wake up and see that the games you used to play meets reality

Hey! Listen!

Because talking is pointless when action quiets the words you'll never speak

Given the power of courage, you'll learn that wisdom is a damsel in distress; and power himself is far from good

In a world full of evils, it's dangerous to go alone

Sword and shield in hand, the challenges and puzzles that lie ahead will defy the warrior within

Some heroes wear tights or masks, but green tunics are different too

But no matter the uniform, power never hesitates to make you face off against monsters and beasts

Training nonstop, eating to survive, and doing anything to find these gems; even if you must smash a pot or two

Because when your damsel is in distress, while your world is seconds from chaos, do you have enough courage to step up?

In a time where you don't have enough time to be scared, can you be the knight to slay off the powerful evils you must confront?

Success can't be purchased

So master defeating all that is evil with the master sword

Endure more hearts than the one you own for full health

Open the chest to reveal the tools to victory and restore the peace

You think you're adventurous enough to handle a tall task?

Can you continue? Yes or no?

Then quickly, let's go kickstart and press start

(2019)

FOOD PORN

If you see the hunger in my eyes, then this should be no surprise

To eat you like a fortune cookie, to see where our future lies

To put this icing on your cake in layers by the pound

And leave you hot and stirred 'til you make a mac and cheesy sound

Save me the spaghetti noodle kisses, that doesn't please my gut

I'd rather please your treats until your crème filled, like a donut

Giving me choices of breakfast, lunch, or dinner and positions that'll get me up

Wanting the best of both, I want you like my eggs, but sunny side up

Flip you like a pancake and let the syrup runneth over

Supply you with coffee because we'll be nonstop, 'til we reach dessert time

You never knew this footlong was so strong

You never knew this steak was more than you can take

But that's okay; box me to-go, so I know I'll be around for late-night cravings

So, let my tongue be the butter to your buns, so I can see you shine like glaze

So, you can continue to serve me this spread, like a Golden Corral Buffet

Just so I can recap this "all you can eat" kind of day

Because the way you sit on a platter, I instantly fall in love with the view you display

(2019)

PSYCHOLOGICAL TEST

Through these eyes are truths in which my mouth doesn't speak

In which my body doesn't react

In which my mind often doesn't want to process

Which then causes me to be numb

Two personalities, one body

Two point of views, one set of eyes

Multiple minds, one brain

Crazy? I am that

Trying to make sense? I prefer not to be

Like a puzzle, I'm not well put together

But when I am, I portray an image

I see a beautifully constructed collage, but some see a mess

But everyone's entitled to an opinion, I guess

This portrait you're reading isn't meant to impress

Because little do you know this art came from depression and stress

And writing this portrait for me was the ultimate test

That me freeing me, through words, was my greatest distress

God has given me a reason to speak without speaking, I can say I'm truly blessed

Now I no longer take little things for granted

I had to see beyond the keyhole view when I finally allowed myself to open the door

But as I countlessly battle a walk with sin and salvation, my mind keeps joyriding through both dimensions

While trying to take care of the generation after me, hopefully they won't see many men within a man

But would simply love and exercise the flaws

Crazy? I am that

Ignoring life's speed limit, my drive is crazy

Heavy footed, the pedal knows me well

Many lanes, but one road, is there a common theme?

That no one lane can keep me sane

I guess cutting off my gas line will be my only slow down

But as my mind runs in circles like a NASCAR track, will eternal love ever give me my victory lap?

My love is all love and all love is my love

But not all love is eternal love

Because other's love isn't true love

So now my love is divided up and separated from other love

So, I must often guess which love am I expected to love

Crazy life, but I'm crazy, right?

I guess the darkest days create the brightest night

To darken the many loveless lives and brighten all love with equal might

To try to define, I'm hard to define

Evolving and transforming, there's a forever encore performance in my mind

No standing ovations, because I'll applaud my mind

Because no matter life's storm, I'll continue to shine

So, if you're trapped in my mind, don't get lost in my mind

My mazes are labyrinthine and provide no light or guidance of any kind

But I'll be watching you because I have your back, so you'll always be fine

Put my together and I'll give you a brain tease

The truth is out there, but can you piece it with me?

Playing numb to life's truth, my mind equates the answers

For once the right question has been asked, some of me begins to be redefined

(2019)

NO DAYS OFF

No days off, no days off

Making power moves, success is the pay off

I don't battle the world, only the time clock

No matter how time is branded, I'll keep moving 'til one of us stops

Working sixteen-hour days with no break

Big checks keeping food in and lights on; I suppose that's the ultimate breakthrough

Dealing with family feuds and family drama, some would consider that a time out

But the mind juggles solutions to avoid the stress; so, the body is ongoing

Too often people I thought were close wanted me to break

But they can't break what doesn't want to be broken

Even my own reflection tries to slow me down

But as a man with my titles, I have inspiration to keep going, so I'm never too far down

Rest? Never heard of it

I guess I'll fully understand when I draw my last breath

Forever up, from the sunup to sundown

Computer like frame, the money is the motive that my storage can't keep contained in my hard drive

Looking forward to me and Jordan having the same amount of money

Knowing we had different earnings, but we can equal the same amount

That the accountant loses track, and with frustration, recounts it

Restless with money, I want my children's children to witness no struggle

That grandpa paved a way when everybody thought I was only good for cliffhangers

I just had to bridge the gap that leads to success on the other side

But so far into the future, the present often keeps me on a leash

That all will come in due time, sleep or not

Even though sleep is needed, because if I don't, the future won't be promised for me

Even if I was at rest, my mind wouldn't; so, the restlessness cycle will resume

Because my livelihood has no off days

(2019)

THE TEMPLE

On Sundays across the country, religion is practiced

Praises lifted, hymns sung, and love exchanged

My religion I once exercised, is no longer working out

The temple I once found peace at, has shown me that neither blood nor water can share the same life here

On the avenue blessed by Maryland, not all blessings flow on that same one way

A big family that's more like a clique, traditions have died well before I could even have made this a home worth joining

The problems the family and I were a witness to, we wouldn't allow it to define us

We hugged, we greeted, we accepted the welcomes

Growing bonds, baptizing lives, and sharing marital flaws

We felt complete, but somewhere a disconnect was spotted and all that was mutual slowly erased itself

The ways of life created many problems, so our lack of attendance grew more visible

Instead of expressing love to assist, people grew cold

Are you honestly praying for us, or only preying on us?

Instead of breaking bread and sipping wine, we're breaking bonds and having to act like visitors due to our broken hearts

Doctrines in Christianity, but it all seems like malpractice

As the preacher preaches on for a change in hope

But the only change will come when we hopefully find a new home

Hurt more ways than one, the seventh day will always be viewed as another day in my eyes

Too many false prophets that gave me life support walked off as I started to flat line

But the love I have in my heart moves on

Just as the love I have for the Temple family moves on

In closing, I understand all have fallen short to the glory of God,

But if it's always reoccurring, are you learning or are you settling for your mistakes?

To avoid all the evils in cliques and all the unsettled ways we've seen

The family and I are seeking peace and pursuing it; that's Psalms 34:14

(2019)

SAFEKEEPING

It's been a long time since I spoke your name

It's been a long time since I heard your voice

The joys and laughter we shared often, reminisce through my brain

But as the casket fell, the tears fell

Unread pages from an unfinished story, leaving the family on a cliffhanger of no rejoice

But no path is an easy one as we all find our own healing

For the bloodshed can be healed, but the scar remains visible

The dreams you once had are the dreams I dream in my dreams

Little clips of what ifs and if only, the end credits never show

But as time makes up for our sad departure, your remembrance takes new shape

For the cousin, I considered a brother, had help me recover rapidly

A father of one, at the time, I was surprised with another upon laying you to rest

So, my heartache was quickly filled in a heartbeat

With him never knowing you, I named him after you

Not to be you, but to be a remembrance of you

To settle the atmosphere, from despair to new opportunities

God's plan is unpredictable

Prayers that were never prepared, provided answers to resolve the worldly hurt one could bare

Decades beyond where you once stood, guide this new life

To soar beyond this limitless sky

And be a witness as his dreams match reality

Lord, let the darkness of my pain create a glow towards a future we never saw coming

To brighten what was dim, to shine upon the shadows of the day

To uplift the family circle, and restore the peace of what was

The memories I have from you are for safekeeping

The name to my son is for safekeeping

But the vault is never securely closed

Because the memories that often visit are never truly locked away

(2019)

THE FRANCHISE

I'm a son of a son

I'm a son to a son

I never want to see my son fall like the sun falls

But to always shine as my son rises and be his mother's sunshine

No need to weather his storm, I'm a storm breaker

Running around the house, I'm a storm chaser

The thunder he claps and lightning he screeches are the predictions I forecast as a news breaker

Despite our storms, the birth of you was like a Superbowl winning drive

Yeah, I may be the coach, but you're my franchise

Your success goes beyond a ring

The dedication to go beyond boundaries

The motivation to stay up even when losses come about

That "everyday grind" I instill in you to progress each day

That every day there's a lesson to be learned to help you, so one day you'll be the coach and not just the player

The tools I'm trying to give you will help you win at life, and not just to manage

That's the making of a true champion

So rise up

Be brave, fear no challenge

My love for you goes beyond the sidelines of your life

You don't have to win me over, you're already a Hall of Famer in my eyes

So, whether I'm trying to weather you, or coaching you, you'll always be my son

The brightest in your mother's eyes, and the brave-hearted man you'll become, your milestones are just waiting on you to unlock them all

I know it's something you'll attempt to do

But you will obtain them all with each grinding day

So never keep your head down, your brightness burns brighter than the sun

Because all these stars are chasing for what you were born with

(2019)

DADDY'S GIRL

Loved by many, but she's a daddy's girl

Viewing people like stars, but I'm her whole world

Mom is the main provider, but Dad shapes her mentality

My livelihood is the rocket that will pave her dreams beyond this galaxy

There's no sense of me without you

I have the whole world in my arms when I'm hugging you

The fears and things that may cow you, will never cause you harm when I'm protecting you

You're my first and a special one at that

With so much love, I know you'll always have my back, just like your name appears on my back

If I am the king, a princess is what you are suited to be

A ruler of rules, but someday you shall rule above me

To shine like royalty, as your reflection reflects a future queen you were meant to see

But queen or not, you'll always address me as "daddy"

Your first words had to be "da-da" to solidify that you're a daddy's girl

No guitars needed for you to rock my world

With you in my life, I couldn't live without you

Born a day after me, you're a special gift for a lifetime

From bedtime prayers, to midair stunts

From car ride jam sessions, to sharing a meal

My vision doesn't go too far without seeing you in sight

I've seen how much we're growing on one another

Our hearts would never need to touch to feel a connection

Because if we hold hands, we'll always spark mutual daddy-daughter love

(2019)

JOKER

I'm an odd man, a different type of human being

In a deck of 52, I stand differently

At times, pain is a horrible price to pay in this game called Life

Little did I know that some pain can be countered with the pain of laughter

So, I guess the joke's on you if you're always taken seriously

Always mad when happiness is the best pursuit

You can't pretend with happy painted face, if your thoughts are always negative

And turn towards torture and violence to doom humans for the sake of your happiness

But I guess not all happiness is defined equally

As some happiness is as small as a knock-knock joke, while others are asylum bed-strapped tear jerkers

Where I stand, I laugh at me the most

Because I know all the things that make me happy

If that means I'm insane, then I know my normality is permanently separated from others

I can always take a joke when others can't, because they love being their own worst critics

So, as I bow from my own one-man show, I ponder if an encore is acceptable

Because whether you're laughing with me or at me, I'll always get the last laugh

Because through pain or hard trials, I know what it takes to put a smile on my face, do you?

Life is only as serious as you want it to be

It's okay to stand out, even if it means you're alone

The ones that laugh the most tend to live longer

So, if you're not smiling enough, then I guess you're not living right

Why so serious?

(2019)

RUMORS

In this business-like society, people forget how to mind their own

Always trying to be an additional shadow when I'm not giving them light

Trying to feed on my soul because their soul isn't right

Trying to plague on my dreams, but I'm up all night

I'll never understand your motive to be so low

I'll always give myself praise even when your confidence is low

I'm my own writer to this story of life I write

If I need a secondary source, I'll keep you posted

Your story doesn't match my story

Too many things in yours that show I really don't know me well

Like water and oil, how can we ever go together?

Your written story is through word of mouth, when my actions are in silence

So, who's true to who?

You've managed to find me and yet you're the one still hiding

I didn't know these were the games we played

Either you loved me and want me to fail

Or you hate me and still want me to fail

But it's obvious I've captured your mind

So, can I call checkmate?

Because it's evident I've won without even playing

In this one life I have, you'll need multiple lives to keep up

This lane in life I've decided to place myself, is only seated for one

I'm sure yours isn't with me

(2019)

PENCIL THIN

When curiosity meets imagination, a love affair grows

I grab you in-spite of

The art in me enjoyed the features in you that exist

No curves needed to get my attention

With that red head no one can mistaken

Loving my hands on you, we draw closer

But if I play too much, you draw the line

When we're together, you manage to read my mind on sight

It's like you manage to know what I'm saying as I say it

And when I'm in the wrong, you always know how to correct me and make it right

Often, I can't figure out who needs who more

But if I don't have you around, can our message be clear?

Me rubbing my hands up and down on you

So much poetry in motion, I hope I don't cramp

Visions written, ideal doodle dates

No matter the occasion, you're always in a sharp, tight dress

Always good at poking for attention

The stories we form, I make sure they can't be erased

With so much more to come, whether I see it or not, we're inseparable

As long as we have one another, we'll always be able to give art to this world that keeps blank pages for you and I to express upon

(2019)

LOVE AT WAR

We break up to make up, the household is in a shake up

Because our bull for each other is starting to get fed up

So, our energy will never be the same, which causes this set up

Cursing, fussing, and crying telling me to grow up

But calm and in composure, you're the one that's blowing up

The nights we slept on angry thoughts

Cutting ourselves to the core

Entering the library of our past

Blowing dust and reopening chapters of our past as ammunition

Keep trying to pull the trigger, but they're all blanks

But somehow, they found a way to hurt

Heart dripping blood, but covered by my chest

Tears rolling down her eyes that make-up couldn't disguise

No matter who was in the wrong, both of us will have to make it right

My daughter hugging on me, my son crying days at a time

They don't know they're stronger than they know

And as I see the potential they are bound to have, I must see for my love life

Because, even with my glasses on, everything isn't clear as expected

But this growing family has the prescription to correct it all

The things that matter most to us is why the fights are ongoing

The care is visible, that's why the frustration is characterized

Love is perfection, but not 100%

So, what in the eyes of others seems hectic, I know is really a work in progress

Tears will become laughs again

Love bends but never breaks

So, if a fight spills, I know it will get messy

But I also know what it takes to clean it up when others expect it to stain over

(2019)

PAY THE TELLER

I keep feeding itchy hands to the people that bare my skin

But when it's time for me to belly up, I'm left starving

Those same itchy hands that get full, get amnesia

Looking at me like an ATM, I expect my deposit the same time you requested yours

Never did I expect to extend my hand for what's supposed to be directed to me

Because now my thought process goes from friendly to aggressive

When friendships get tested because of a problem I choose to help you resolve when I didn't have to

Trying to help people struggle less, I see I must change my humble mind

The blessings and fortunes I have, I want to help make a difference for people

Not trying to be like Oprah, but I want to create a little hope

But I see now I'll just pray for you, before I offer an offering

Because the little lane I gave you to help you cruise, you took as a highway joyride

(2020)

THEN & NOW

Looking into a two-sided cracked mirror

I'm reflecting separate images

Of what I am now from what I used to be

As I continue to look deeper and deeper, I'm given footage of what I am from what I once was

I remember when I was young going through boyhood

Adventuring in the forest, pretending to play hero and beat the bad guys with my childhood friends

Now I'm in fourth gear into adulthood while lost in the jungle

Tangled up in the thorns trying to find the path that makes the most sense

I remember the days when I ignored church and grew tired of Sunday praises

That the darkness I'd rather see was my eye closed shut and dreaming

Now I'm constantly fighting the dark to seek the light that I've had on hold so long that speed dial no longer connects

I remember back then all the girls I've ever done wrong by

The sadness I probably never saw

Now, my first-born I can never attempt to disappoint, because her smile is everything

So, when I close my eyes to sleep, I already know my daily dreams have met reality

Back then, I remember the days my cousin and I challenged one another in everything

Mainly because we never saw eye to eye

But still, I never knew if I wanted to be more like him, or he wanted to be more like me

Now his death comes too soon

Naming my son after him, the tears he wishes he could shed, I'm wiping from my son's eyes

I remember the days when I thought I couldn't find the one that matches all of me

That my dreams would help me create the one I'd consider my whole world

Allowing TV to boost my imagination as acting consumes my reality

Now I see my flaws that my childhood eyes weren't prepared for

The beauty I'm now blessed with in a wife

Ignoring my conscience, I went with my heart

The love peaked with highs and lows; I can truly say I'm happy for her impacting my life

The challenges we'll face we shall achieve them all together

I've seen what lazy days used to be like

Drawing and gaming life away for days at a time while my world stayed between four walls and a bed

Now every day is a day to improve

Up like money and Vegas lights, trying to capture the day when money chases me

Fighting to flip rent money into a mortgage

Eyes are red as hell, but sleep only occurs when my wife makes me stay still

We're forever under the umbrella that doubters rain down on us

But we loved our social distance from others well before the world understood the coronavirus

So, whether the mirror is cracked or brand new, my image is in a consistent change

From what I am and what I used to be

The things I've learned, battled, and conquer will always define me as my film of life is still ongoing

For the day I finally can say "the end", I want to know I've done more good than bad

And the things I either feared or regretted, can be overcome and applauded with a "well done" praise

(2020)

TAYLOR SON

With every loss, paves a lesson

With every win, more challenges come

But no matter the wins or losses, it all equals to wisdom

Wisdom I want to pass to you

A prince in my eyes, that's no puzzle to me

But you're one piece of many puzzles, so you're never puzzling me

But to the outside world, you're different, so they always seem puzzled

But when they finally piece it all together, will they really see how special his piece, and all pieces, are to me?

From baby to toddler, someday the things you used to hear helps you to listen

That the things you say, others play deaf to

But with the help the family strives to give you, will help you heal the ears of many when your voice becomes crystal clear

Remembering the days I made money just to burn money

The things I bought had no value

Now I see I must provide better so the money I make now helps you to increase your future wealth

Planting you like a seed, I expect you to grow

As you root and grow, you manage to catch all the dreams that fall under the sun

So that when retirement suits me well, you'll provide your mom and I all the shade

This poem cuts deeper than what was mentioned in Ava's eyes

Because you were both born the same, but with a different mindset

Learning to go the extra mile for you all, nothing will keep us at a distance

Granted, Ava is as beautiful as an oil painting, her attention doesn't compare to the exercise you give me daily

The many chases I must do to have you smiling daily

I just want you to always look up to me

And when you have your head down, it's only because I have you lifted in the air

I know you give me fits, but there's nothing more fitting than being your dad

A franchise player in my eyes, I'm just trying to coach you up

The learning curve is a wide curve, but we're at the mound; we've got to swing it

I hope you manage to understand

Because as you continue to learn your numbers and shapes, I'm trying to stay number one; because I'm forever around

(2020)

ENTERTAINMENT

The wolf tries to lick his wounds clean to better lead his pack

Hunters all around him; trying to take aim like a target on his back

Attempting torture to see if his bones can bend until they snap or crack

But kill him where he lies

Because his charge will be stronger than any gun's ability to kickback

Entertainment, what are you wanting out of me?

Trying to binge me on TV, like a Netflix series, they dying to see

Trying to degrade the best me I can be

Just so viewers can critique or laugh, when there's no money coming in for me

But if I change up one time, I'm acting funny

Certain relatives take me for a joke, so I must be funny

Playing on my family, you must be nutty

Remembering the days you needed us most when your rainy days weren't so sunny

Even though we got your backlash from the people that

did you cruddy

We still gave you love, damn, how'd we get the label of a dummy?

That money came up, so no food became soul food

And those things you could never get, eventually came with a receipt

Months go by, the family calls to see if all is good

Just to find out y'all wanted to play amnesia on us in a silent heartbeat

Couldn't figure out why a childish mind was in an adult

But the family had to fall back just so our blessings and success could be discreet

Because you'd rather push people down for a better come up

So, whenever y'all decide to call or send a text again, just know I'll be sleeping well

Because the bull you're trying to serve to me won't sell

We've entertained one another too long, this chapter needs to end

Because this chemistry we had was oil and water that wouldn't blend

(2020)

WRITER'S BLOCK 2: LOW INK

As time goes on, I write

Situations, problems, scenarios; pen made it to paper

Ideas came and went whether the pen kissed paper

Writer's block keeps clocking in and out like a full-time job

Frustration brews around the clock

Motivation and inspiration in unicorn rare

But as I continue to write, am I still making sense?

Are my dots still connecting?

Is my drive still there despite low fuel?

Ideas, thoughts, and topics pending, but can I manage to write it out before my pen runs out?

The addiction and adrenaline to write in younger years are no longer the same now

Some of life's problems weren't writing as it once was

The love and passion aren't the same now

Desires and consistency became a flickering candle flame

I guess you can say I'm a trick candle

So, when I fooled you, I fooled me too

To think this gift I have can truly go away; even after all my resources to help me burn have disappeared

So, whether I'm a Chevy classic running on diesel, or a hybrid running on electricity, I'll always have a drive in front of me

No matter the speed or gear I'm in

Whether I'm driving on the highway or making the highway, I still have a lot more miles left in me

If the world is in my vision, I'll always have something worth writing

So, write I must

(2020)

HUMBLE KARMA

Pending your attitude

The patience is wealthy

Trigger pulling is unscheduled

Targeting a growing family

Praying for the best, expecting the worst

Your professionalism is sin

The family is blessed and lavish

The protector praying over his upcoming generation, but hardly for himself

The shield can never sword

So, he allows God to strike as karma

Bearing the cross, they've crossed the wrong family

The bottled rage can only pour out love

Only because, that's the right answer, when the human in us all is to strike like lightning

Karma slowly coming down like thick molasses running down a tree trunk

When it finally touches down, it will be well deserved

For the uproar you tried to create to a humble loving family

Can you taste it?

I'm sure the diabetes can as it numbs your ligaments to the core

Your untimely shots only grazed

But karma's aim will never miss

The outcome can't be sadness

Because this is the expectation you didn't think would come

Peace, love, and happiness is all the world needs

So, when you step beyond these boundaries, karma will make you fall back in line

So, don't try to finesse if the energy you give, you aren't able to receive

Lesson learned

(2020)

HOME FREE

The rent money, I had to flip that

Now I have keys to a mortgage knowing I won't rent back

Leaving the past and problems at my old door mat

Because my new location is a fresh new start from the old flashbacks

Too many times I had to leave my family, for work, in conditions I couldn't laugh at

People trying to break in from the front, while others getting arrested out back

Neighbors yelling night after night, storing drugs under the floormats

My babies pointing out mice in their rooms, causing more problems and setbacks

Announcing this to the leasing office and they just swept it under the floormat

So, out of frustration, a true home I had to find; that would be the ultimate answer back

So, as I watched drugs and fiends walk around the neighborhood, that was once peaceful, I kept saving and working hard

Police and fire trucks racing through my avenue, trying to keep the peace, while the family worships in the churchyard

Now my end results have my feet up; watching the kids play in the pool in the backyard

From watching houses get raided, and transactions in my front yard

To watching the wife planting flowers in the front yard

Allowing my family to see a promising future was my ultimate trump card

To have a home and invite new memories, so life can be a little less hard

So many goals in front of me, I just check one box at a time

The mountain is infinitely tall, but still I climb

Still young to this game called life, but tired or not, every day is a new day to reinvent my prime

As long as the lights are on, it'll be time to showtime

(2020)

MORE LIFE

There must be more life than this

These bills, these kids, these challenges

Looking for more life

I know I'm living, but I wake up daily knowing I'm inching closer to death

Hit after hit while thinking

Exhaling my soul and thoughts through my nostrils

Cooking my brain just so my fingers can run through the clouds

Temporary distractions from stress

Trying to crack the code to life and unlock peace

And ask peace why every trail must I endure hardship

Always strategically making sure my dominos are lined up perfectly; never to fall

But friends and family I positively try to surround myself with, have other intentions

Life is as wide as the ocean

And I was Titanic ready

Not knowing life would give me too many obstacles that would potentially make me sink

Anchoring me down as my brief life flashes before my eyes

Breathing in water, I see the air bubbles swimming to the top

Fighting to keep this one life, like a video game

Maybe if I prayed more, I wouldn't mix my faith in business

I know faith without work is dead, but I've worked so hard, I'd allowed my faith to vanish as my success progressed

Hard-headed and stresses in all directions, it's hard to think

Thinking if I'd cut my dreads that'll help, but it just helped to grow more headaches

Young with so many years ahead, I live knowing that better times are ahead

That the loved ones I'm surrounded with are the best supporters

And that God's love is just the turn of a page whenever I need a good reading

As much as the world forces itself upon me, it's a test of who I am and what's to become of me

Only then will my faith grow, and stress will be better managed

Which then equals more life

(2020)

WHY ME?

I'll never understand the things that people do that make them want to lie

To hide the truth of realty just to lie with false promises

Whether they'd be strangers, close friends, or family

Nevertheless, I'm always in question if every statement said or done is accurate

Because people are consistently inconsistent with accurate facts

It seems nowadays I feel like I must wear a bulletproof vest just to protect my heart

But does it really work when they keep aiming for my head?

Because even on a good day, somebody has a lie already in the chamber

Ready to cock it back and blow my mind

Oddly enough, I'm more reluctant to have my head blown off, than to be stabbed with the truth

I guess the world I live in today would rather me be dead inside, than to patch up a bloody wound

The truth can be the easiest, keyless door to open if people allow themselves to do so

But instead, people would rather cover the door with brick wall

Hoping it's secure enough to stand the test of time

One stick of dynamite is all that's needed to blast the truth open

So, in the end, was the door even worth it?

The truth is never easy

But the truth is real and needs to be heard

In 2020, the truth only seems to come out when someone is wearing a mask

Protecting their identity because no one is raw enough to confess without the fear of shame from the world

The world has suffered for far too long

It's time to dig up the truth that's been buried under lies and half-truths for so long

And reveal the facts of the unknown

Only then will the freedom within us be unchained

(2020)

SMALL CIRCLE, LOW BLOWS

When I said, "I do", I gave forever to the one I love

As challenges consistently come, forever stayed forever

Certain times forever was questioned if it would remain forever

But I redefined the doubts and remained dedicated

But certain friends and loved ones in my small circle consistently gave me doubt

To make me change my vision to match their views

To potentially end working progress; and cut short a good story

Every love story can't be the same as the rest of the world

As flaws come and go, love doesn't judge or point to blame

So when loved ones give me grief and point out the shame, I continue to hold to my wife and kids that I claim

The trails I walk, I carry the pain

The speed of life is never steady, but I stayed in my lane

Because when my destination is met, I'll look back and smile at the one's that challenged my love as I create miles between us

While they saw dead ends, I saw more miles behind the signs they never crossed

So, as I keep boxing with life's opponents, I assume my smaller circle would be coaching and cheering

But some would rather step in the ring to try to prove a point

But if they thought I would be going down swinging, well I'll be sweating it out round for round

So, I can make you into a believer, as my body of work goes beyond twelve rounds

(2020)

COLD TURKEY

I'm no longer tapping on a vein to jump

I'm avoiding injecting more sin that I'm trying to reject

I tried to play it safe

I tried to manage the signs

Kept covering up my prints, but like a criminal, I kept getting caught

Trying to save myself from the law, but she's always in the know without my say

Addicted to my sins, but wanting a fresh start, I walk in circles

Wanting to pull away but wanting to stay put

The battles off and on became wars, and still I fought alone

People try to view me, but I'd rather keep my lights off and blinds covered as you try to view my house

Medication seems so easy to take

But when I think I've sobered up, I'm feeling light years ahead, when it's merely minutes as I relapse once again

My outer appearance is smooth and subliminal, while my mind and inner character are cracking like a mirror

I can only assume why I can't see a clear image of what's to come of my future

Because I'm so lost in the cracks of my addiction

I want to prove to myself so bad that I'm better than what I've characterized myself as

But I keep proving to myself I'm still the same

Even the law is tired of the same old crimes

I'm on the verge of jail time that I might not come back from

In the house of my own

Cracked mirrors and all, I have prepared for battle that'll make its way to war

To help medicate and sober permanently

The only question is, is the permanent temporary?

I guess that's the subliminal help I call out for when I continuously choose to be alone

(2020)

PURIFY

Love is free forming daily

But my greatest enemy is the reflection reflecting back at me

The state of mind I battle to showcase for the future, often has a hard time shaking the past

Like cobwebs, I can't brush them off

Like a scratch, the past is itching for attention

Like the good times can't last always, a brief intermission

Visioning a bright future, but psyched by a dark past, has lackluster my mind's intuition

But the heart is where it belongs and can hopefully inspire the mind to reveal its holiness of ambitions

Old Me:

Doing big things, how long is this going to be?

Own car, good girl, two kids to add to your family

Too many times I've seen you slip and seen you try to live more lives than given

You must be your own loser because you keep yourself from winning

You want more out of life, but are you willing to do more?

Often procrastinating and quitting too often

When you know life will keep adding more

Are you sure this is what you truly want?

To be the man that runs the show

To me, you're still incapable of success in which your dreams begin to haunt

Stuck in a child-like fantasy with nowhere to go

Adulthood life bearing on your shoulders, can your weight weigh it out?

Because too many times I've watched you, from your reflection, allow depression to set in

Taking shots of lust and sin

The cycle spin of the double life love loss is the cancer you love and hate to fight

So, don't let your clothes tumble dry, just air it out

You're just better off staying in the past

The pain is less, and the responsibility is rare

Life was easier

New Hope:

The past is in the past

The new page of a new day is the present I gift myself daily

As I stretch my hands to the most high, I can't change

what once was

I can only learn and move forward

Each test I've been given has been a long road journey of learning curves I continue to endure

As much as I reminisce about what I used to do, that can no longer apply to what I'm currently doing

A man of God, I'm still a child in his eyes

The sins I cast upon myself are forgiven when I truly accept forgiveness within myself

To be a better man and father to the family I bare on my back

The weight of them will strengthen me for the endless journey ahead

Never to look back

Because if I know my past is behind me, I can see that it won't look the same as I take each step into the future

(2020)

DEAR MAE

I've had a lot of other figures in my lifetime

The grandest mother of mothers, I guess that's why you're called Grandma

Through all the ages and stages, you've always been there

Even now, I'm a man, husband, and dad; and you're still guiding me along

Not that I'm doing anything wrong, but you always make sure my best moves were the right ones

Thinking back how weekends we were at Grandma's would be fun while Mom was busy

Laughing at all the craziness I now see my kids display

You'll always be the apple in their eyes

Remembering the phone calls that lasted for hours at a time

How I broke down plans, dreams, and goals

Always finding a way to speak God in every conversation just because it was needed

The little things I took for granted as a kid, have now paved the road that you've taught me to drive

Now I'm ballroom dancing with the sharpest tux, demonstrating proper etiquette with high class

The obstacles and devils in my life tried to hold me down

The guidance you gave me helped me surpass

All the things you've done for me, I can't count them all like the stars in the sky

The love you've shared with me is like heaven on earth, you've always been an angel in disguise

(2020)

ENTITLEMENT

Two kids later, five years in, do you still love me?

Because when bitter hardship interferes, we feud in disagreement

Pride shields us both as we search for entitlement

Trial after trial I look at me, at us, and the pain

Because too many times we've watched each other walk away through a rain-covered windowpane

Driving for miles, clearing our heads, needing a break

Raging for speed as therapy, but stuck at long lights with our foot on the brake

Hour after hour we stay apart, feels like the last goodbye

Our hearts are better than this, but our minds are on standby

So instead of talking to you, I sit here and write

When we should be fixing the flaws instead of possibly debating who's wrong or right

I just want us to return to normal as day turns to night

Because I've been your best protector, as if you're the castle and I'm the fearsome knight

Fighting for us, always, and keeping your eyes from forming any kind of tear

Because I still love you and value you as the highest in my top tier

So, don't let every big or little fight we fight make you feel like we're through

Because I know it's in the moment, but after a while, we'll get through

As our kids play and cling to me by the waist

I look at the happiness we all present, and see that the bitterness we displayed was a complete waste

That if we lessen our pride and come up with more solutions, that'll be our greatest lesson

Because deep down inside we not going anywhere; we're forever joined at the seam

We just need to hug and pray more, because our situations aren't as serious as we make them seem

Whatever foundation is broken, I'm willing to put back together piece by piece

If it means all is restored as we continue to explore the pleasures of our peace

(2020)

REMEMBER ME

I told her I'll make you remember me

But the pitch I gave, she wasn't swinging at

Little did she know I was beyond second base

I'm on my way to making a homerun, so win or lose, I'm bound for a score

The bedroom is our playroom

If I'm the playground, then she'll slide down

Going up and down, I only wish she saw the view I can see

Swinging back and forth, the lust is airborne

Bed driven; my meteorologist poked out some scattered showers

As her thunder thighs begin to shake, our platform began to quake

Reciting my name like a teacher doing roll call, I'm well attended but never early

These "scheduled workouts" are beginning to work out

As you spot me, I bench you, the sweat is to be expected when you know how to make it come

Building stamina through cardio

Watching you yoga, to stretch it out

When it's time to cool down, we'll only heat up

Because when we're in the sauna, we'll be the reason it's steamy as the glass heats up

Like a detective on the scene, if you name the place, then we'll have a case

If we're outside, you're the bird and I'm the bee

If we're in the car, then you're the ignition and I'm the key

One motion, and you'll be turned on easily

If we're in the kitchen, then you'll see how we precook

And if we're in the bathroom, you'll think we're out in the ocean as I give you some splash play of this boat hook

So, no matter what you do or where you go, I'm earlobe inches away

All you must do is hear to know I'm here

Signature your body with my tongue all fancy

Laminate these memories so you can always remember me

(2020)

FREE GAME

Sleeping on my success has been a dream come true

I've come out of dreamland and put in the work so those dreams can remain cage free

Now I'm money savvy, avoiding jails, and have my own property

Playing it close like monopoly

But before the titles and success, I was young and thinking I had the game mastered like a mastermind

But the reality of it all was that I was moving one piece at a time on the checkerboard, when everyone else around me was making chess moves

So I had to take a risk

Had to play operation on my mind

So, when I was told to stay within a board to achieve minimal success, I had to break the ice

Slowly, I started waking up from my dreams

To form ideas by adding ambition, commitment, and to remain dedicated; that's how I learned to connect four

Because if I want my money stacked like Jenga, then I'd have to deal with a few twisters

Bound to build on my net worth, I had to remain hungry, hungry if I want to get all I know I can take

Treating all competition like battleship, I'd expect trouble to sink in

As I continue to soar towards success, I knew eventually everyone would abort towards the chutes and ladders

Because their commitment to knock me down was greater than chasing their own

But now you don't need a clue to see who's on top; just guess who

Sorry if you thought it'd be you

Better days are ahead as I treat every day like a payday

The mouse traps and jeopardy that tried to plague me couldn't attempt to match; even if we played apples to apples

I've striven to the top until I am numero uno

Trying to keep from getting scrabbled in this game called Life

I only ended up being the game winner

(2020)

ZOMBIE SHIFT

Normally you expect everything to be done during the day, but my money is to be made when everyone's asleep

Money goes on and on, I suppose you can say my race starts when I'm clocked in by ten

But not every job is the best job, as I feel like I'm walking to my own grave

As night becomes day, I leave the graveyard feeling like a zombie

I work before work during the day; so in return, I fight my sleep as I work at night

Balancing responsibilities with husband-daddy duties, I've worked a sixteen-hour shift before I've clocked in and do a regular eight

So, when the supervisors think it'll be great to work an additional eight

It's hard to process that in my head when I'm mentally dead

I've been up counting all the stars, so my mind is somewhere in outer space

Walking gingerly with a thousand-mile stare

The moon is bright, the night is cold

I'm all clocked in, but working like a zombie

As the money piles up, my sleep diminishes

It's like the lights are on, but nobody's home

Tired is almost taboo when the expectations are so high at home

Bills need to be paid, mouths need to be fed, air and heat needs to keep flowing

So, if money never sleeps, then I'll always be in second place

Yawning comes every now and then, but that's as close as I'll get to sleep as my watery eyes close for a few seconds

So, just know I'm dead during the day, but resurrected at night

Feelings are lively when I'm paid in full every two weeks

Working nonstop as the humanity within becomes zombified

So, if I ever do go to sleep, I might really be dead

(2020)

YEEZY TAUGHT ME

I'm not sure what it is that started it all, but often I wonder

Was it that I discovered Jesus Walks before religion?

Already knowing there's no church in the wild

Or the fact that we both share June 8th

But I've followed your career and let it take life unto me; and looked at you like a big brother, knowing I'm an only child

Good morning, as my early childhood stages lifts off

Living the easy school life before the college dropout

Because while you were breathing in and out, through the wire, I was simply trying to keep a smart mind while in the school spirit

Young minded, I allowed all of the lights and ultralight beams to play out my childish thoughts

Deception was the real monster I never knew about

Because while I was young, nobody could tell me nothing

While nearing the peak of my childhood, graduation was the new movement

But far from my own graduation day, I began discovering some real friends

Enjoying the homecomings, flashing lights, and the glory of it all

While you were rapping about home, I was far from my own

Partying with drunk and hot girls that could barely hold their liquor

As memories of the night began to fade, we all were in search of a new day

Early adulthood started off amazing

Graduated, working, and had my license in no time

Life was moving fast, but I had to drive slow

Listening to you more and more, I began bumping slow jams and crack music at the same time

The street lights and I were getting to know each other more and more as the music played; it became our newfound addiction

The adulthood cruise I saw only had two words, "No end"

But little did I know I was being welcomed to the jungle

And it was too early to celebrate

A few years go by and a few relationships were tested, but I met someone gorgeous

Still young and in love, I said "I do"

While I was getting my ring band and love lockdown, you were going through the high and low lights and letting the world know that you were a God

None of it made sense at the time, I could only assume it was some type of guilt trip

But I paid it no mind, because at the time all I could do was feel the love for the girl I love

But as life presented challenges, so did the sin

Testing me to see what I was bound to do

Dark fantasies began to crawl into my mind

A different type of power that the devil in the latest dress presented to me

To help me see the other me, the Gemini side of a beautiful dark twisted fantasy

Everything was hands on

The fire we made every hour made us stronger

No water could cool us off

But this hell of a life I never expected was no longer the good life when I was caught

Heartless at the time, I welcomed the heartbreak

Even though she wouldn't leave, I still look at it as bad news

Only because she could've found better

But instead I've decided to follow God

Only then I would feel free; because at the end of the day, he would be everything we need in this time of healing

Song for song, it's shaped a story of mines

Album after album, we've evolved and managed to become better men

Many think that you've lost your way; that they miss the old Kanye

But I'll be a fan regardless, but never to say I'm number one

As I wait for more albums to come, I know I'll love it before I hear it

And as the haters continue to judge and critique, I know no one can stop your love; because Kanye will always love Kanye

I just hope it finds its way to help me continue to take shape of my life

For all the love and dreams I continue to pursue

(2020)

TAKE FLIGHT

I want to fly

I want to fly to my dreams that still seem so far away

Far beyond the clouds and deep within the stars

Give me the chance I need, and I'll take flight

To fly so high, that I'll no longer see solid ground

Higher than any weapon could shoot me down

The lane is clear, my chance is here

Fueled up, ready to accelerate

Zooming far beyond the expectations and doubt

Landing on this intended dream, but not staying forever

For I have many dreams to soar to

So, as I keep my wings extended and the wind under me, I'll forever fly

For infinity

(2020)

PEACE FOR RANSOM

People nowadays in 2020 are so miserable, that instead of them trying to build you up, they enjoy seeing you fall

A sickening illness that's more killer than the coronavirus

So bad that now the peace I once had within myself is now for ransom

Offering service, time, and blood to others doesn't seem to be enough to have what was once mine

That others will continuously bring me down no matter how much good I do

That no matter how much praise I embrace, people will still pray on my downfall

Having pages upon pages of things that I've done to positively impact myself or my family, but would rather look at the list of things I've done wrong in my life

How can I tap into my third eye if I'm stressed with no peace of mind?

Everybody has an opinion that I need to listen to

Because if I do it my way, it's frowned upon

No matter if the blood is thick or the water is thin, they both drowning me in drama where freedom used to be

Because some claim to love you, while others are hateful

But I've encountered many that simply love to hate me when they barely know me

Thinking they know my whole story, when they can barely read along

So, as I keep searching for both freedom and peace; I thought befriending liberty would do me some justice

Instead I'm being restrained as the fight for my possessions gets even tougher

The new day to day living consists of wearing a mask

To protect myself from the many unknowns

As I fight daily to keep my identity away from the world, I'm trying to restore myself

Too many times I stared in the mirror and saw myself crack while my reflection never chips

Wanting to punch the mirror repeatedly so we both match, but the tearful blood that'll come out my hands are the trills people want to see me display just to label me as something that I'm not after being robbed of my sanity

Very few answers coming my way, God I turn to you

To grant me the serenity to accept the things I cannot change

To encourage the change I can make happen, as my wisdom strengthens

Living out one day at a time, and enjoying the little thing moments

And finally, to accept all hardship as my road to everlasting peace is steadfast

(2020)

Motivated to Help

My size 11 feet aren't everybody else's shoe size

The shoe-filled stories of others I may not truly understand, but still wanting to read along

Still young to this game called life, I've managed to stay one hundred and earned hundreds even when life only gave my cents to change

But either rich or self-rich, I'm motivated to create inspiration in others

But life is no one-man race

Everybody can generate their own standards of success, without needing a finish line

Even if it takes me giving the homeless my last dollar, as they search for their first, I will give them that to help survive and uplift towards achieving more

I'm sure it's all worthy of being viewed on social media

But I do what I do just because; I don't need internet fame for doing a good service

Pure hearted, I would never want to see my surroundings fall or remain neutral

I push, talk, and promote elevation and growth

So the depressed can discover motivation

And as that expands far and wide, all the world can be a

better outlook of positivity instead of where it currently stands

Because when people discover obstacles they can't surpass, or can't find a way or a solution to a problem

It'll be those moments when I truly smile the most and walk towards those challenges

Making a way out of no way and making sure that the things that can't be resolved, will be

Far from perfect, I push for perfection

For myself, and the people I consider friends and family

As they push others to do the same

So, the world can struggle less, and love and encourage more

(2020)

DEPRESSION

The things that are displayed will never be viewed physically

The way things may come off so smooth, you'd never know the battles and storms that are mentally endured

The hurt and sacrifices are religious and often don't feel like blessings

Overcoming, achieving, and winning at the things, that's to be expected, but something still seems missing

Up all night, the body rests, but never sleeps

Things running through my mind that hasn't captured answers yet

As suicide is I.V. inserted into my brain, sadness clouds the mind as rain creates a gothic gray atmosphere

Shielded with a strong smile, the brokenness within is a puzzle that's hard to piece together

With all this money surrounding me, I struggle at times to figure out what I'm worth

Have I given my best at life when opportunities came?

Always judging self, the reflected image rarely speaks positivity

So my end result is a hot serving of loneliness with something quiet to sip on

Never knew this state of mind would bless me with my first poem, but it's therapeutic

To ease my mind, as I test this newfound artist within me

To finally find an output for the things I hold within

And search on for the things that are waiting to be discovered

(2010)

THIS IS IT

After all the things we've been through, this is it

Writing every emotion and thought that I've imagined and encountered

This is it

I wrote when I was sad, happy, and in anger

Writing time after time, giving titles to every situation; this is it

Poetry, you've given me a voice on paper

The ability to free my mind, when I thought my mind was chambered

You have become a drug to me that I've abused repeatedly

And will always relapse to

At times, I even found myself to fall in love with you, when I thought I could never get myself to love anything

I may think this is the end, but I know for sure that you have more to offer me

And when that day comes, I'll be writing more and more of you

But for now, this is it

(2012)

WELL DONE

I am a sinner

I let it be known to God

I pray that the next day is less sinful than yesterday

As I lay my head down at night and rise again in the morning, I am presented a new day and a new opportunity to better myself than what yesterday displayed

I am a work in progress

As I continue to love my wife and kids, I know that they will forever see a man that wants more out of himself and his life to share with them

Having to face judgement, stress, and drama outside of his home, the family is fully aware that this world isn't safe for any of us

That we all must pray daily

That we all come back to one another at day's end safe and healthy as we did when we first departed that morning

God,

You present me many trials and many tests day after day

I will continue to thank you and to live and breathe through every trial

From boy, to man, to husband, and now father, you've guided me in the direction that is destined for me

And even though I'm still learning, growing, and maturing, I thank you through prayer that you've never changed up on me

As I think, reflect, and reminisce of what I once was, to where I am now, all I can say is thank you

Despite the wrong I've done by myself and towards others, that I'm still here and that you're still watching over me

Far from perfect, I still aim for perfection for the life I still have to live out; and to live knowing I have children that hold me in high regard

To make sure they live and aim for perfection as their lives continue to unfold as well

Through all the things I've written in this short span of life I've lived thus far, I can truly say I've had quite the adventure; but still have many more adventures ahead

I only ask that you continue to strengthen me and increase my faith so I can continue to be the best me I can be for the family I have to lead and protect

I've walked many miles

Through trials and blessings

Continue to help me walk on for many more trials ahead

For the love I have in my heart for you and my family

To help guide me if I walk off the track you've paved for me to walk

And continue to help me strive and achieve all that I wish to conquer

So, when my final day of rest comes, I've left no stone unturned in my lifetime; and you can look at me and say well done

Amen

(2020)

www.ingramcontent.com/pod-product-compliance
Lightning Source LLC
Chambersburg PA
CBHW062159080426
42734CB00010B/1748